EASY PIANO

TOP HITS
OF 2019

20 HOT SINGLES

ISBN 978-1-5400-6461-5

Visit Hal Leonard Online at
www.halleonard.com

Contact us:
Hal Leonard
7777 West Bluemound Road
Milwaukee, WI 53213
Email: info@halleonard.com

In Europe, contact:
Hal Leonard Europe Limited
42 Wigmore Street
Marylebone, London, W1U 2RN
Email: info@halleonardeurope.com

In Australia, contact:
Hal Leonard Australia Pty. Ltd.
4 Lentara Court
Cheltenham, Victoria, 3192 Australia
Email: info@halleonard.com.au

CONTENTS

BAD GUY

Words and Music by BILLIE EILISH O'CONNELL
and FINNEAS O'CONNELL

Moderately fast

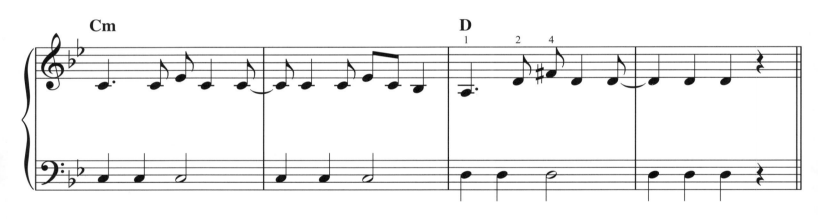

White shirt now red: ___ my blood - y nose. Sleep - ing, you're on ___

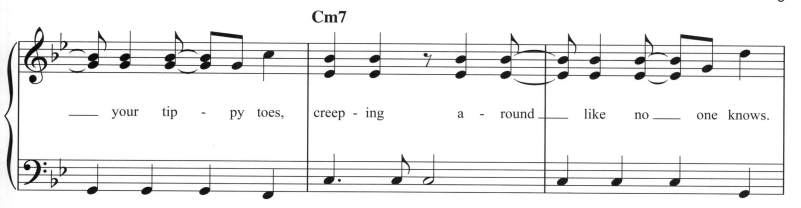

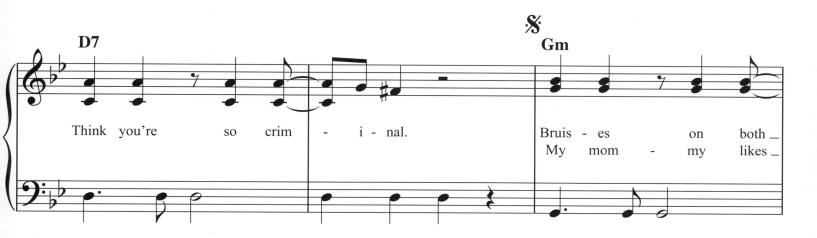

Cm **D7**

I'm the bad guy. ___

To Coda ⊕
Gm/D

Duh. I like it when ___ you take ___ con - trol.

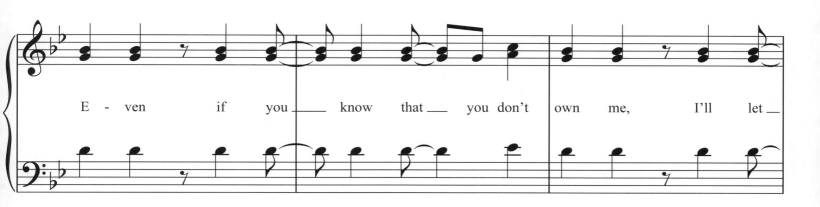

E - ven if you ___ know that ___ you don't own me, I'll let ___

D.S. al Coda

D7/C **D/A N.C.**

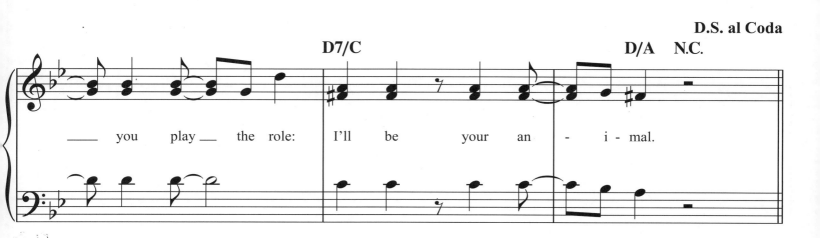

___ you play ___ the role: I'll be your an - i - mal.

8

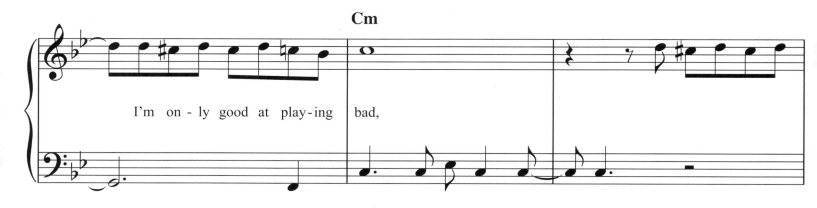

I'm on-ly good at play-ing bad,

bad.

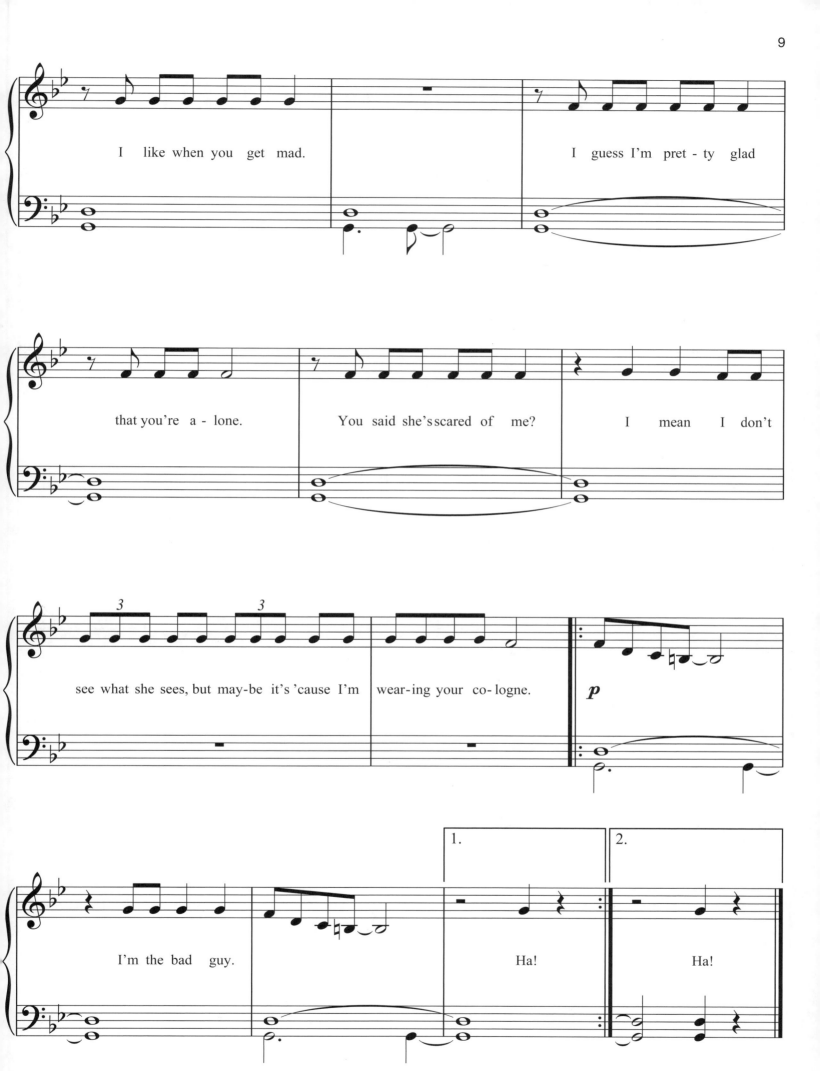

BREAK UP WITH YOUR GIRLFRIEND, I'M BORED

Words and Music by ARIANA GRANDE,
KANDI BURRUSS, KEVIN BRIGGS,
SAVAN KOTECHA, MAX MARTIN and ILYA

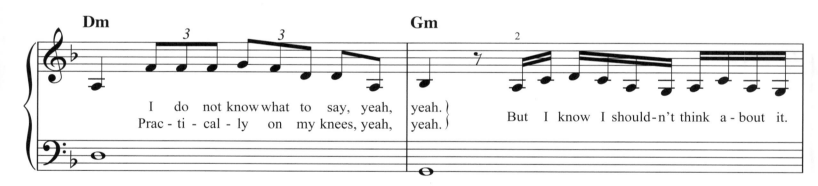

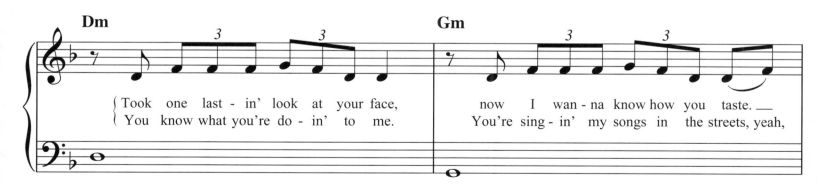

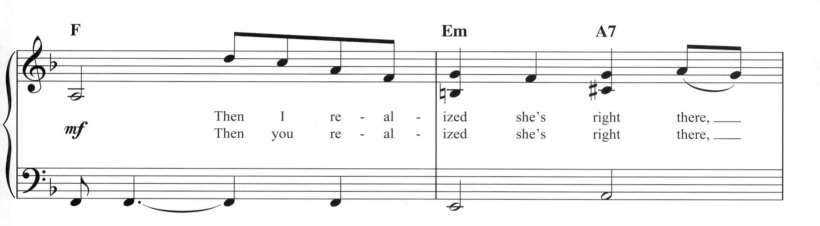

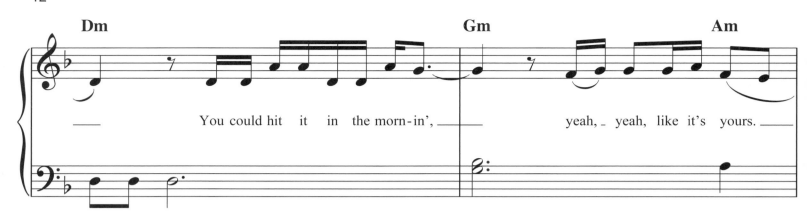

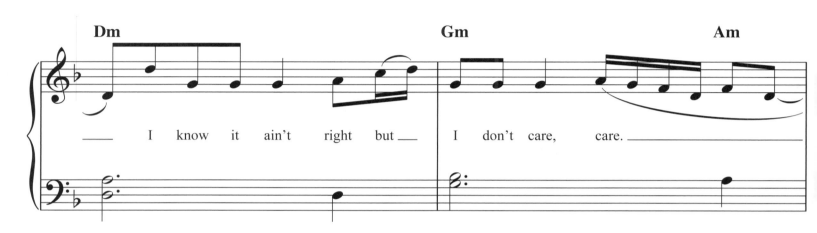

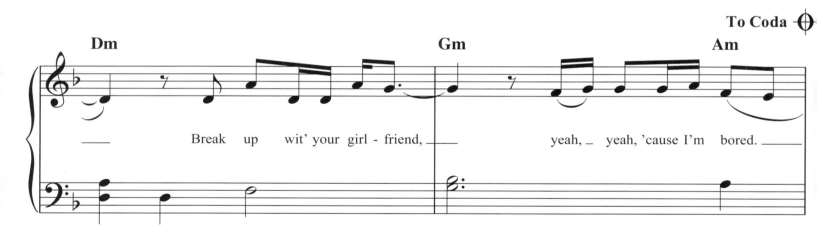

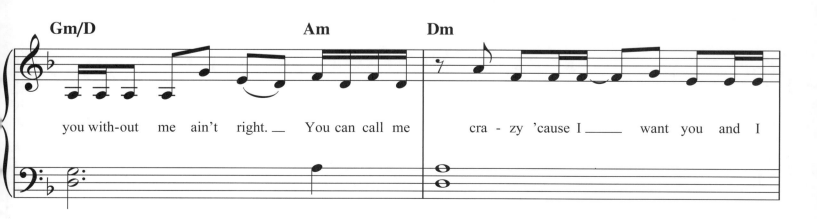

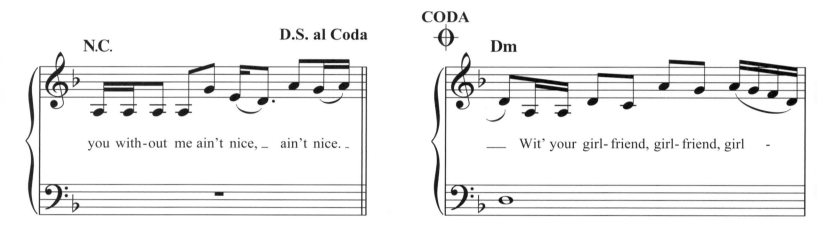

CLOSE TO ME

Words and Music by ANDERS SVENSSON,
SAVAN KOTECHA, THOMAS PENTZ,
ELENA GOULDING, ILYA
and KHALIF BROWN

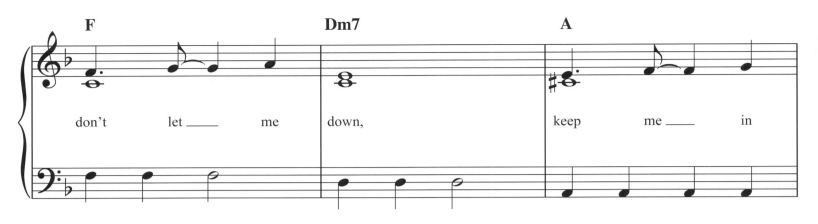

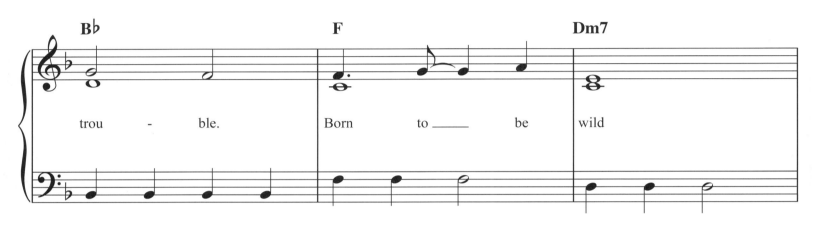

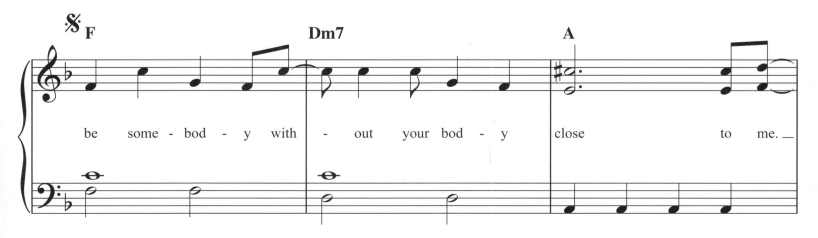

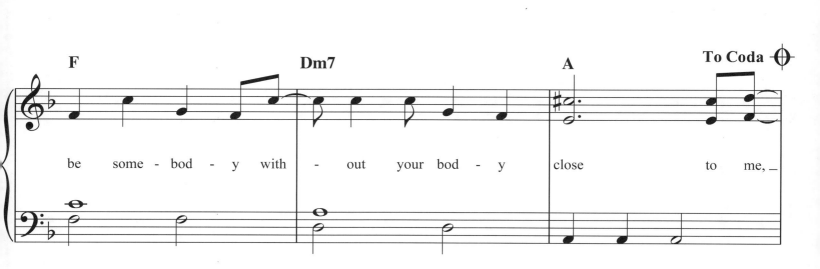

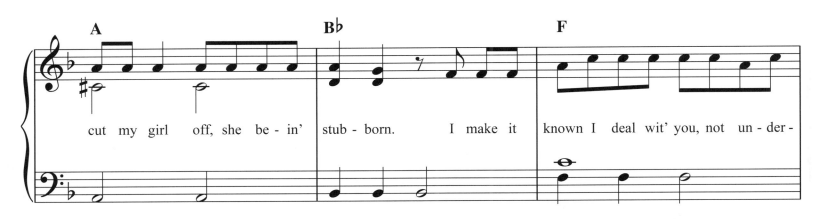

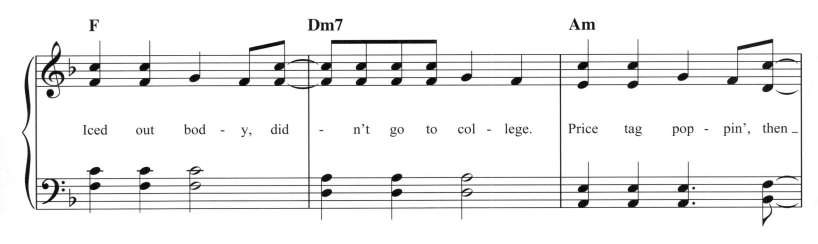

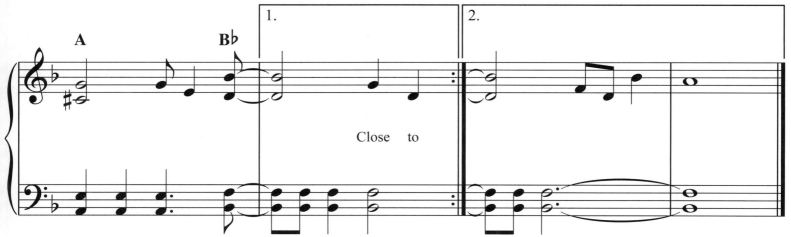

DANCING WITH A STRANGER

Words and Music by SAM SMITH,
TOR HERMANSEN, MIKKEL ERIKSEN,
NORMANI HAMILTON and JAMES NAPIER

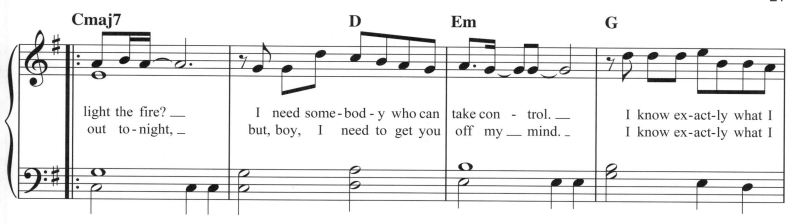

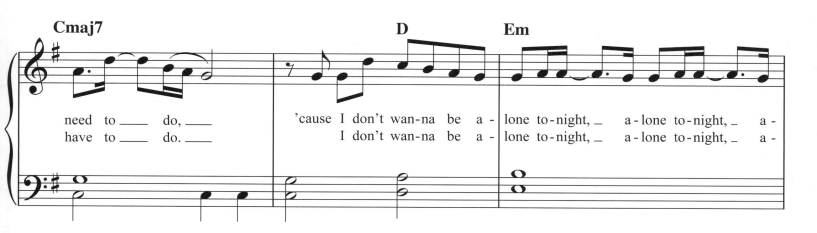

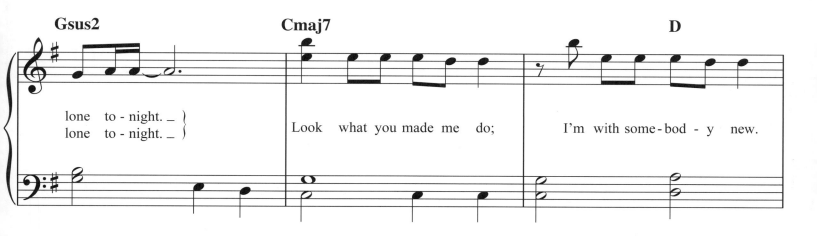

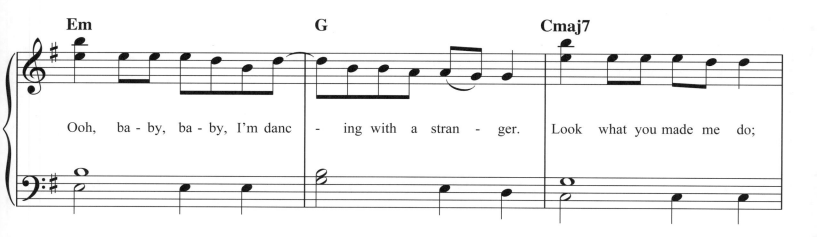

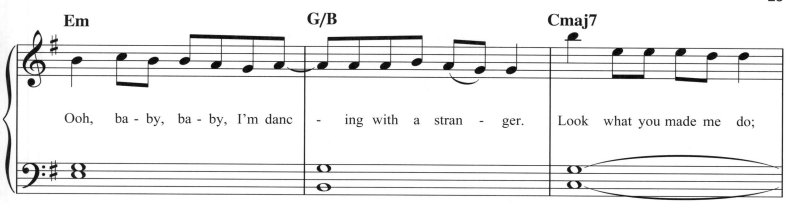

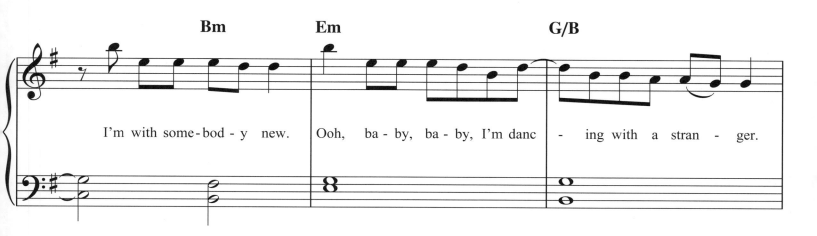

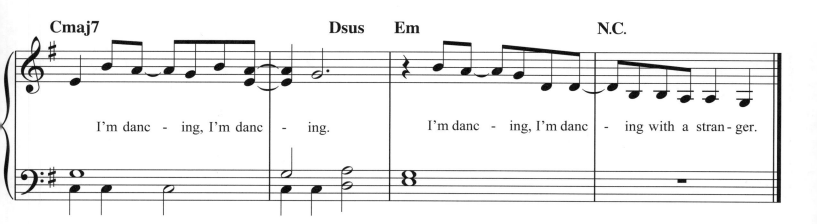

GLORIA

Words and Music by JEREMY FRAITES
and WESLEY SCHULTZ

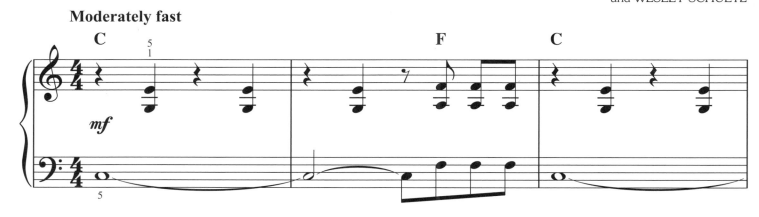

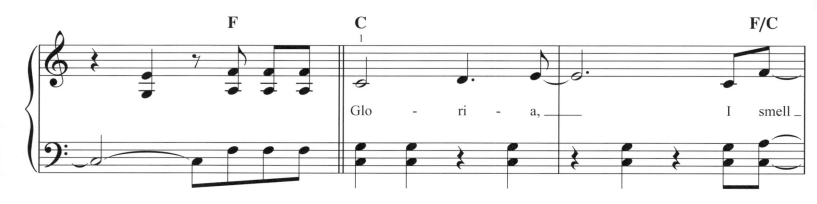

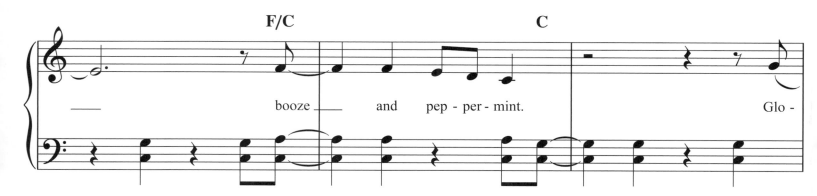

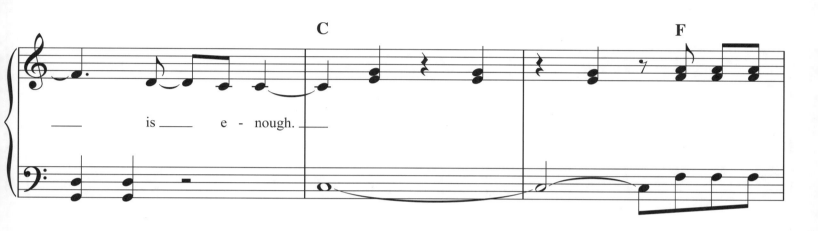

Glo - ri - a, ____ my hand ___ was tied __ to yours.

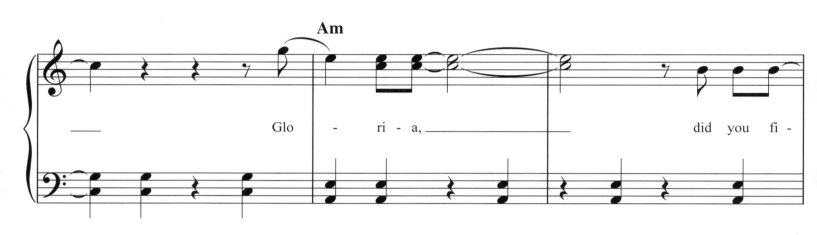

__ Glo - ri - a, _____ did you fi -

- n'lly see __ that e - nough __ is __ e - nough?

Did you know ___ me when? I was young - er then.
Heav- en, help ___ me now. Heav- en, show ___ the way.

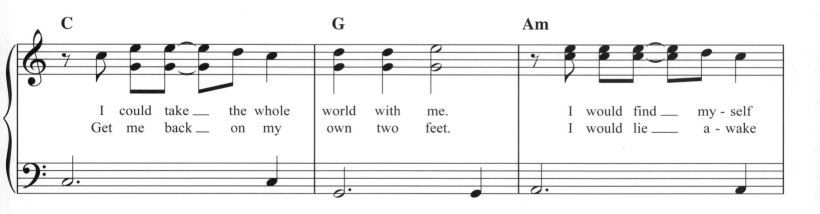

I could take ___ the whole world with me. I would find ___ my - self
Get me back ___ on my own two feet. I would lie ___ a - wake

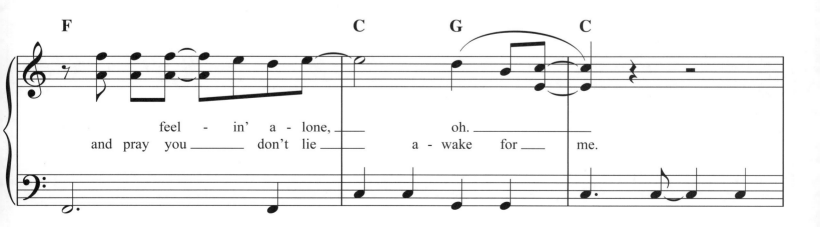

feel - in' a - lone, ___ oh. ___
and pray you ___ don't lie ___ a - wake for ___ me.

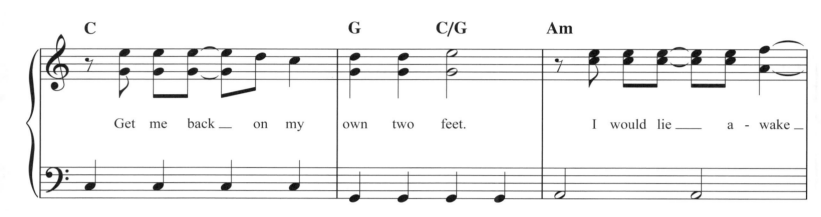

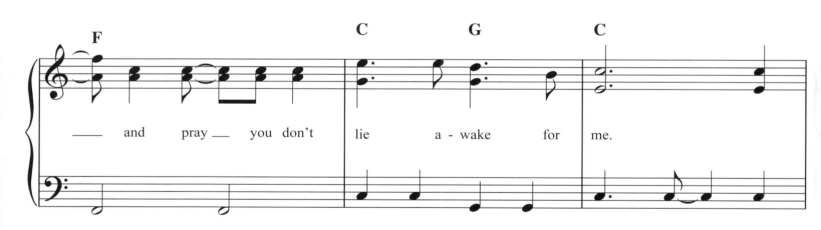

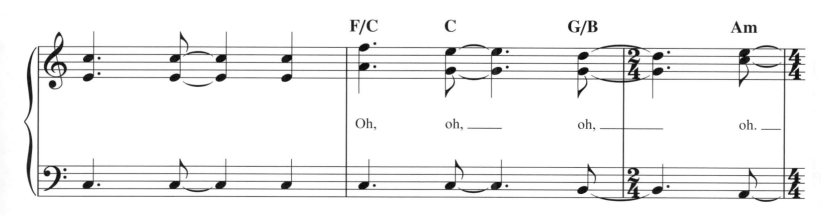

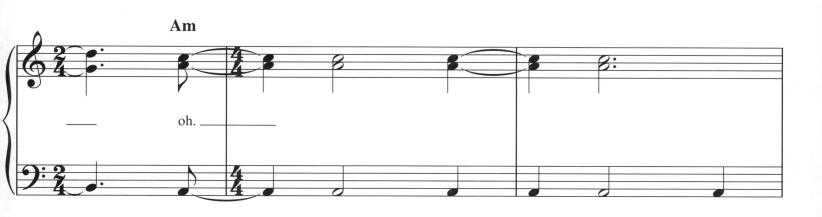

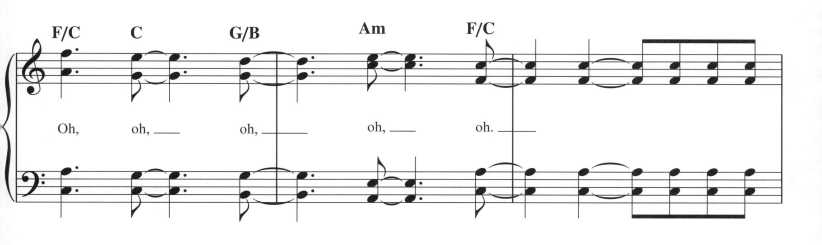

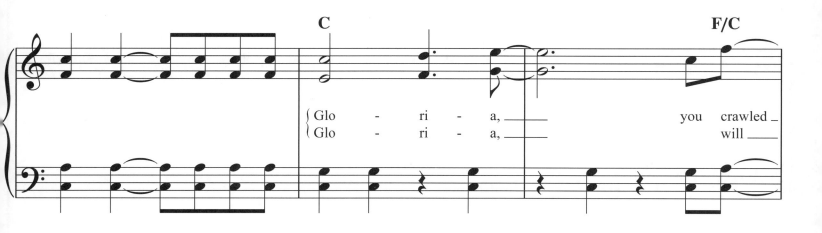

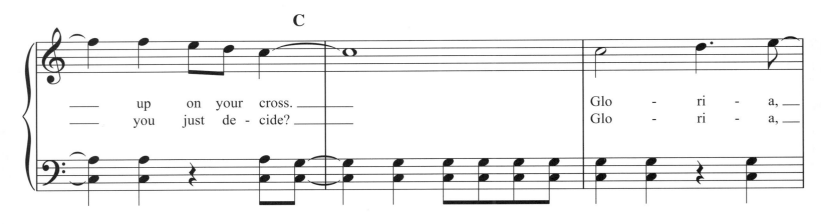

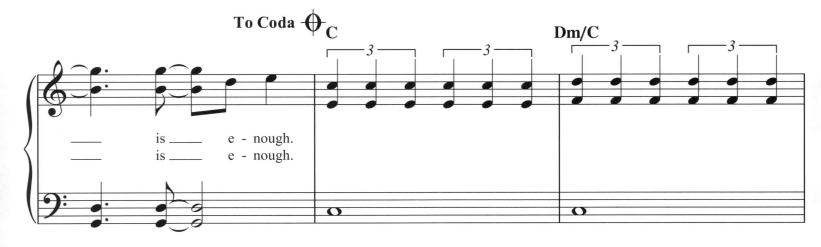

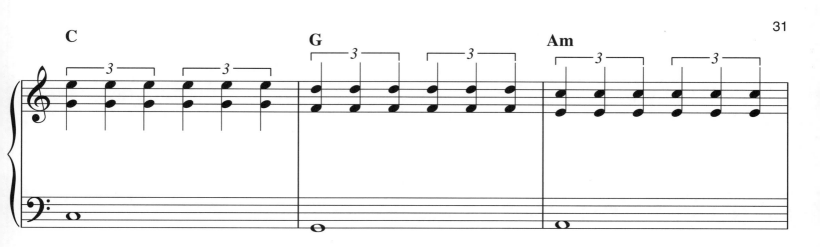

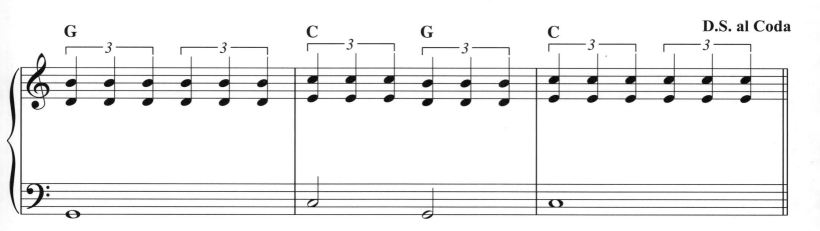

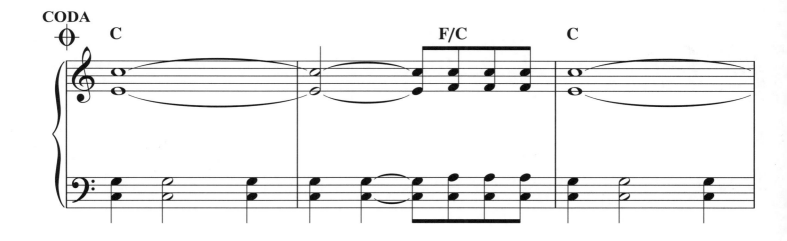

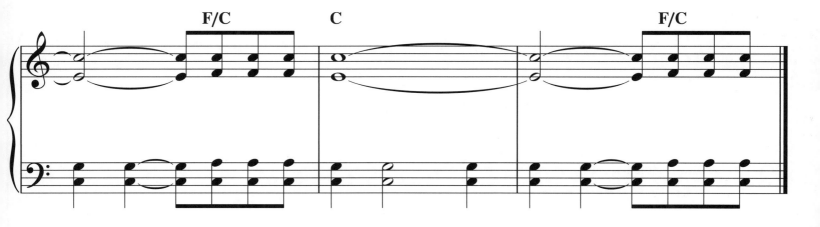

I DON'T CARE

Words and Music by ED SHEERAN,
JUSTIN BIEBER, FRED GIBSON,
JASON BOYD, MAX MARTIN
and SHELLBACK

Syncopated Pop

I'm at a par-ty I don't wan-na be at, and I don't ev-er wear a suit and tie, __

yeah. Won-der-ing if I can sneak out the back. No-bod-y's e-ven look-ing me in my __

eyes. And you take my hand, __ fin-ish my drink, say, "Shall we dance?" Hell,

yeah. You know I love you; did I ev - er tell you? You make it bet - ter like that.

Don't think I fit in at this par - ty. ___ Ev -'ry-one's got so much to
Don't think we fit in at this par - ty. ___ Ev -'ry-one's got so much to

say, yeah. _ I al - ways feel like I'm no - bod - y, mm. _
say, yeah. _ When we walked in, I said, "I'm sor - ry," mm. _

Who wants to fit in an - y - way? 'Cause I don't care when I'm with my ba - by,
But now I think that we should stay. 'Cause I don't care when I'm with my ba - by,

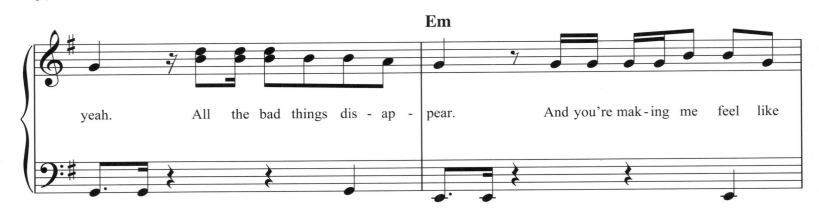

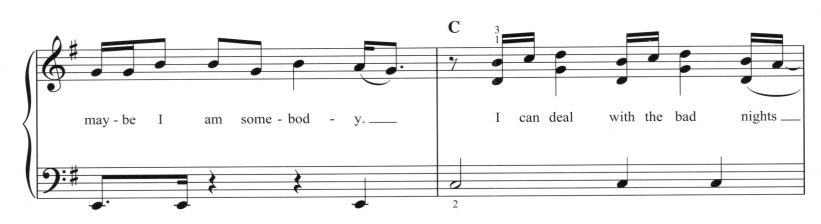

And you're mak-ing me feel like I'm loved by some-bod - y. —

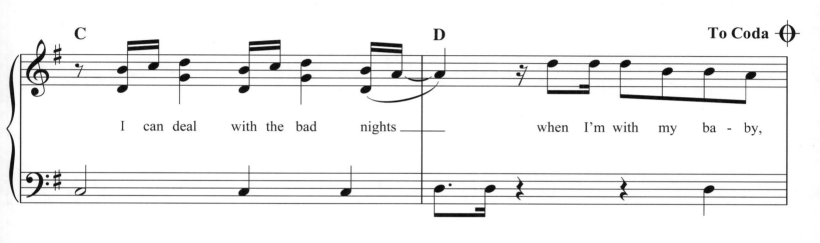

I can deal with the bad nights — when I'm with my ba - by,

yeah. Ooh ooh ooh ooh ooh — ooh. —

We at a par-ty we don't wan-na be at, tryin' to talk, but we can't hear _ our-

I don't like no-bod-y but you. It's like you're the on-ly one here.

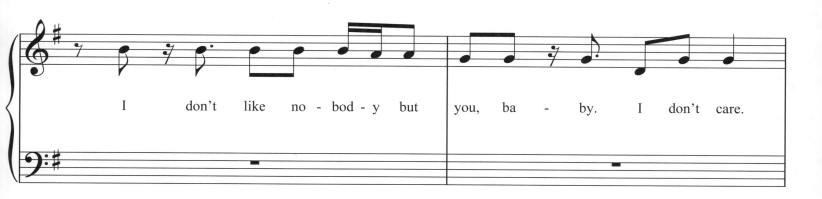

I don't like no-bod-y but you, ba - by. I don't care.

I don't like no-bod-y but you. I hate ev-'ry-one here.

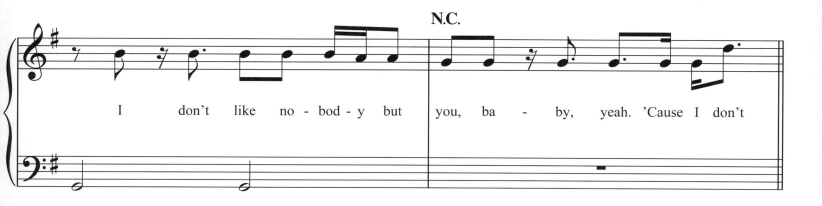

I don't like no-bod-y but you, ba - by, yeah. 'Cause I don't

7 RINGS

Words and Music by RICHARD RODGERS,
OSCAR HAMMERSTEIN II, ARIANA GRANDE,
VICTORIA McCANTS, KIMBERLY KRYSIUK,
TAYLA PARX, TOMMY BROWN,
NJOMZA VITIA, MICHAEL FOSTER
and CHARLES ANDERSON

Slow, half-time groove

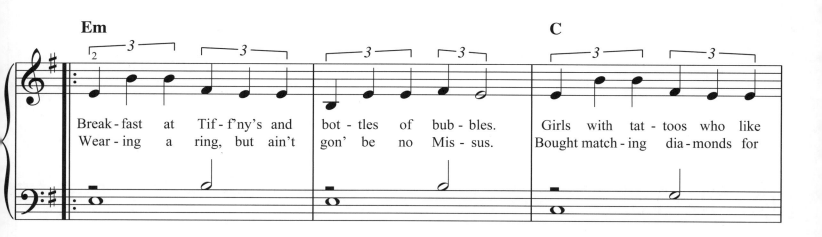

Break - fast at Tif - f'ny's and bot - tles of bub - bles.
Wear - ing a ring, but ain't gon' be no Mis - sus.

Girls with tat - toos who like
Bought match - ing dia - monds for

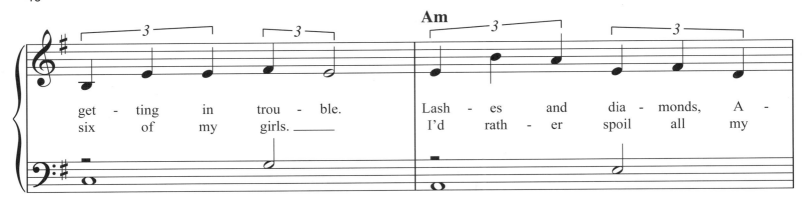

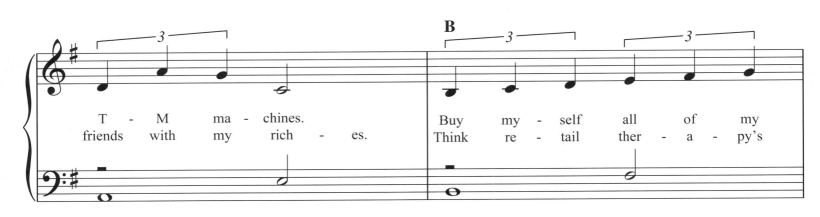

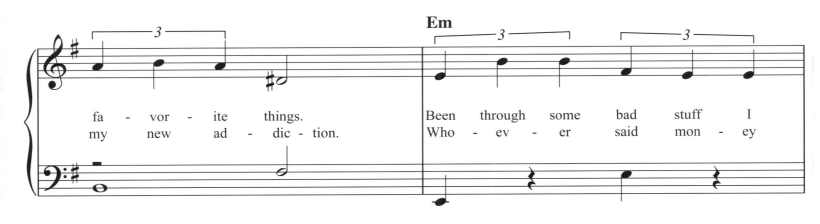

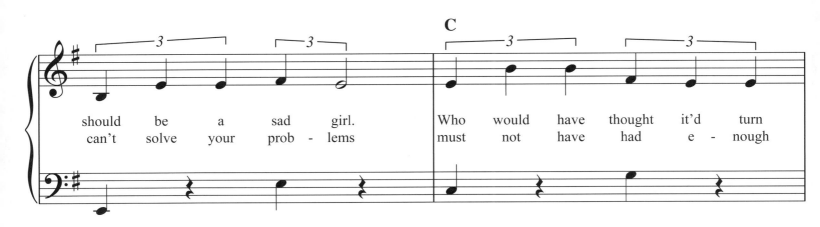

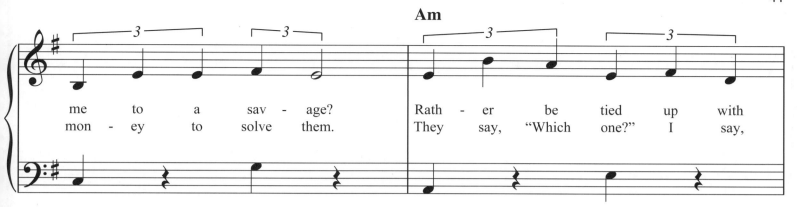

me to a sav - age? Rath - er be tied up with
mon - ey to solve them. They say, "Which one?" I say,

cuffs and not strings. Write my own checks like I
"Nah, I want all them." Hap - pi - ness is the same

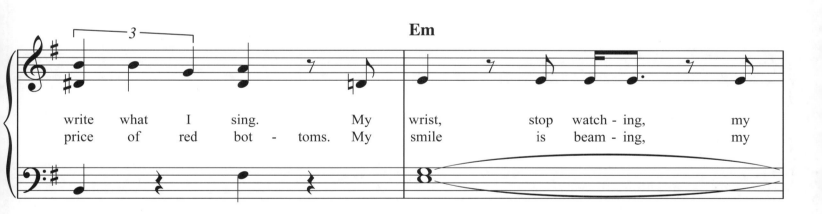

write what I sing. My wrist, stop watch - ing, my
price of red bot - toms. My smile is beam - ing, my

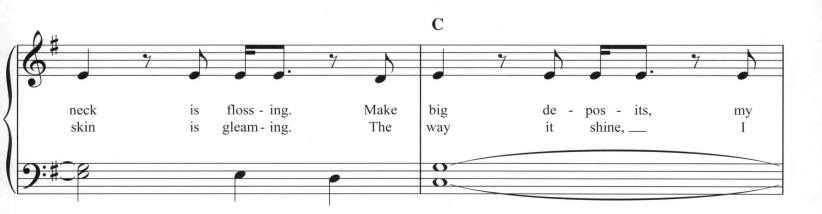

neck is floss - ing. Make big de - pos - its, my
skin is gleam - ing. The way it shine, ___ I

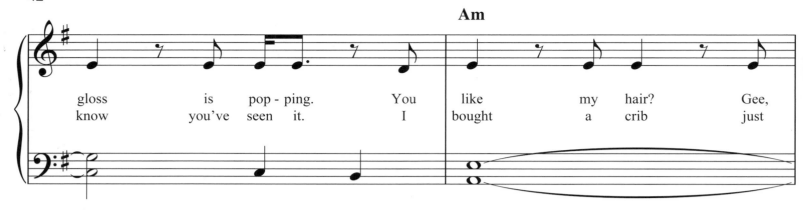

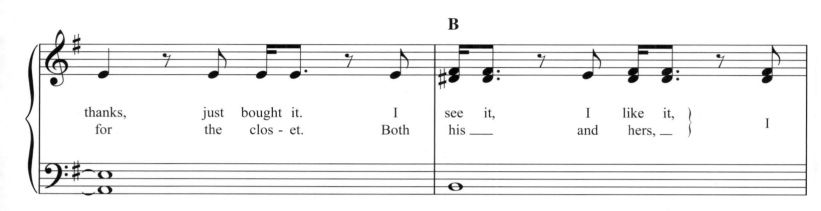

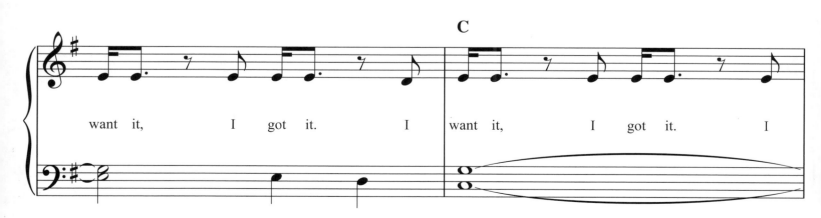

want it,   I got it.   You like   my hair?   Gee, thanks,   just bought it.   I

see it,   I like it,   I | 1. want it,   I got it, yeah. | 2. want it,   I got it. My re-

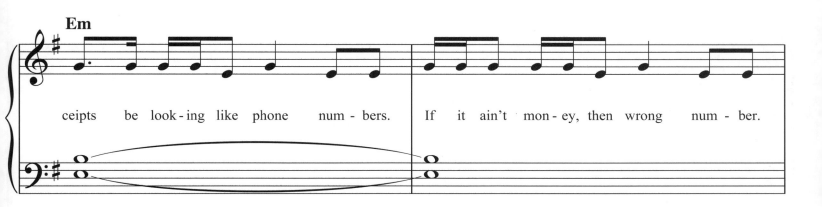

ceipts   be look-ing like phone num-bers.   If it ain't mon-ey, then wrong num-ber.

Black card __ is my bus'-ness card, __ the   way it be set-ting the tone   for me.

I don't mean to brag, but I be like, "Put it in the bag," yeah.

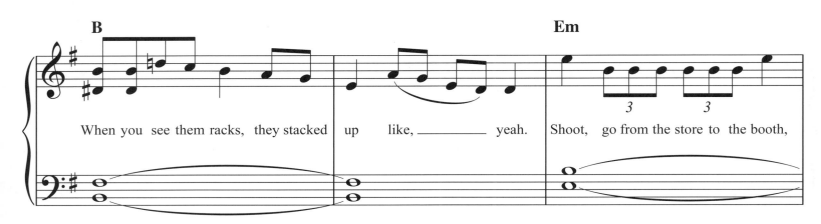

When you see them racks, they stacked up like, _____ yeah. Shoot, go from the store to the booth,

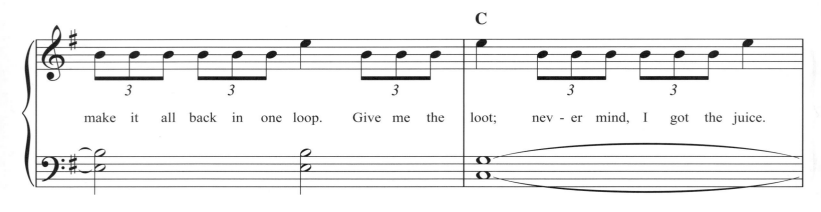

make it all back in one loop. Give me the loot; nev - er mind, I got the juice.

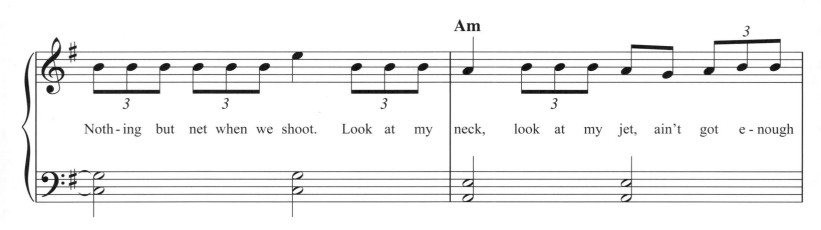

Noth - ing but net when we shoot. Look at my neck, look at my jet, ain't got e - nough

mon - ey to pay me re - spect. Ain't no   bud - get when I'm on the set. If I

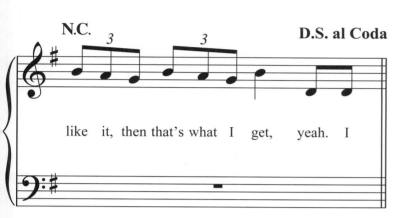

like it, then that's what I get, yeah. I

like it,   I got it, yeah.

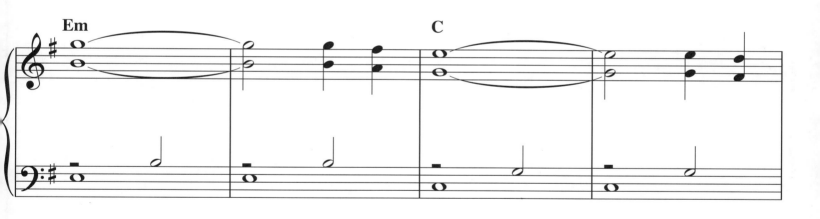

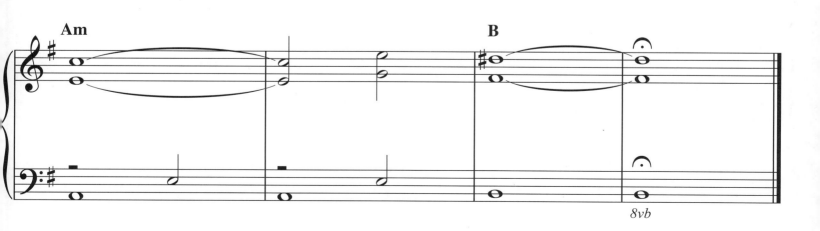

8vb

IF I CAN'T HAVE YOU

Words and Music by SHAWN MENDES,
TEDDY GEIGER, NATE MERCEREAU
and SCOTT HARRIS

Upbeat Pop

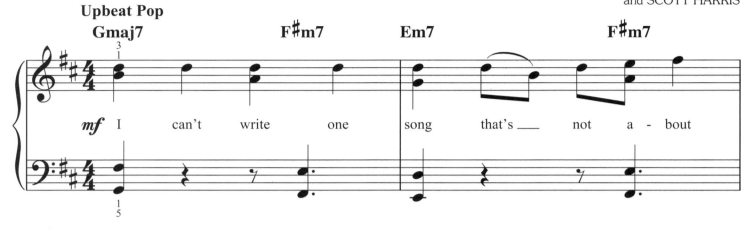

I can't write one song that's ___ not a-bout

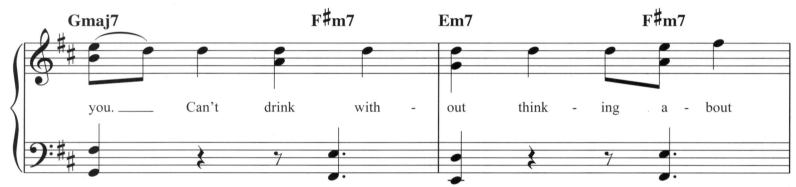

you. ___ Can't drink with - out think - ing a - bout

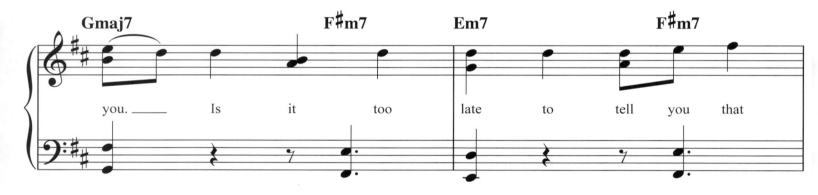

you. ___ Is it too late to tell you that

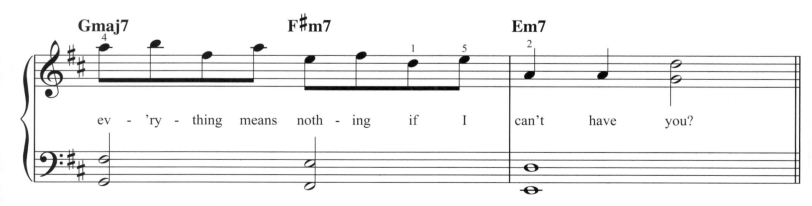

ev - 'ry - thing means noth - ing if I can't have you?

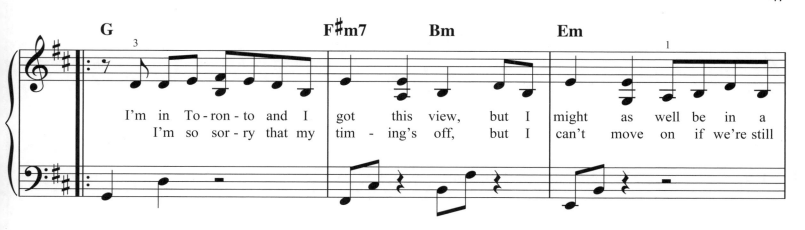

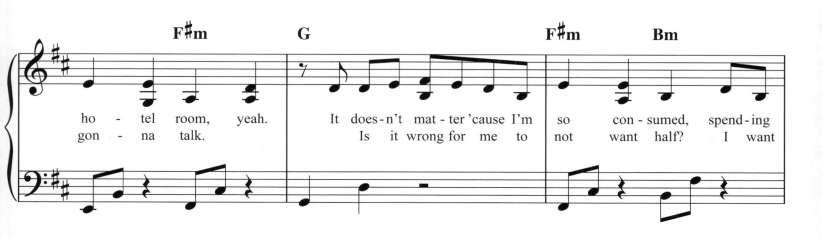

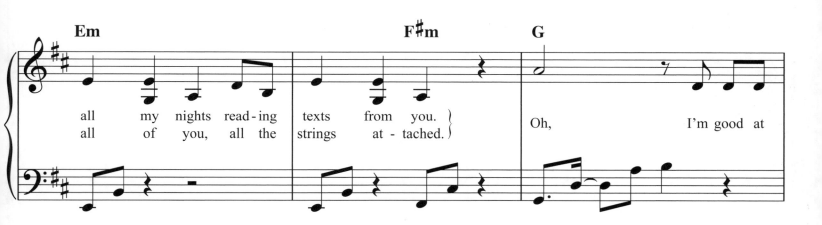

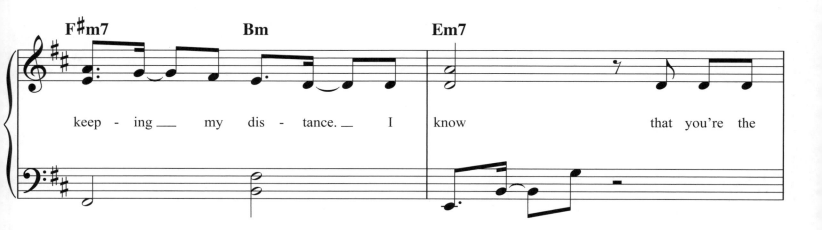

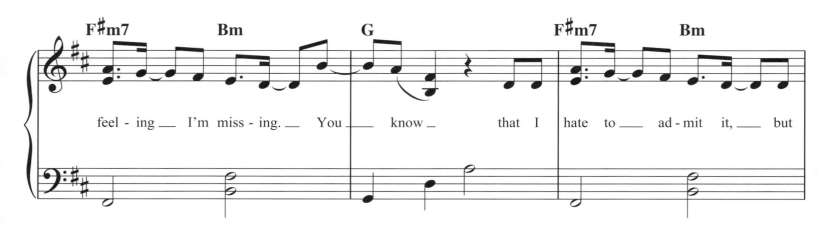

feel - ing __ I'm miss - ing. __ You __ know __ that I hate to __ ad - mit it, __ but

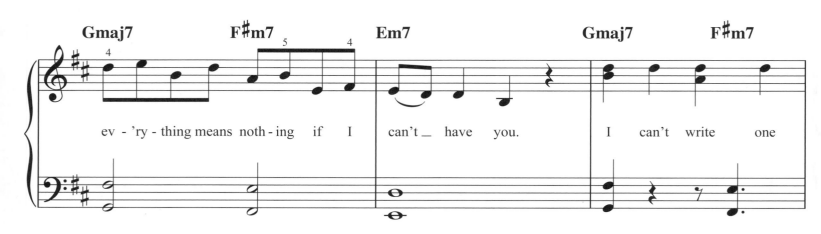

ev - 'ry - thing means noth - ing if I can't __ have you. I can't write one

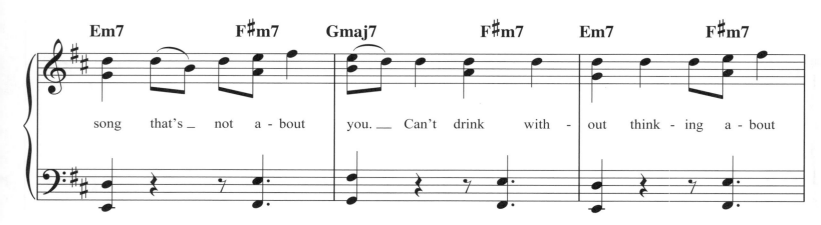

song that's __ not a - bout you. __ Can't drink with - out think - ing a - bout

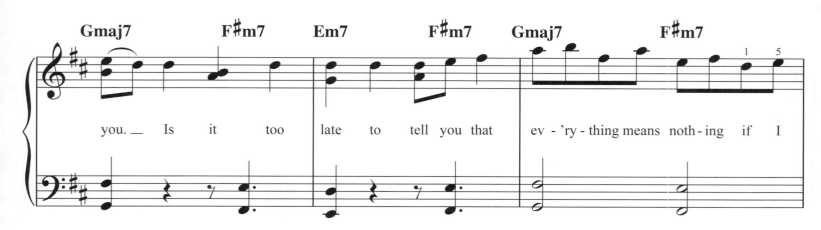

you. __ Is it too late to tell you that ev - 'ry - thing means noth - ing if I

can't have you? I can't write one song that's __ not a - bout

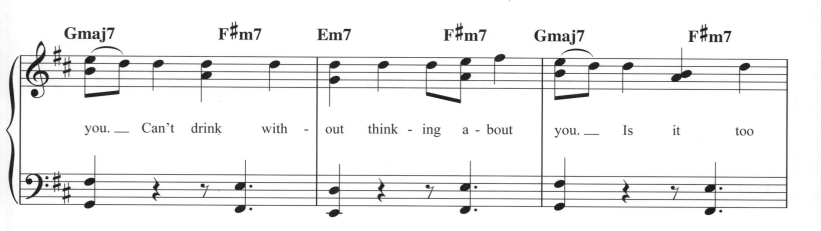

you. __ Can't drink with - out think - ing a - bout you. __ Is it too

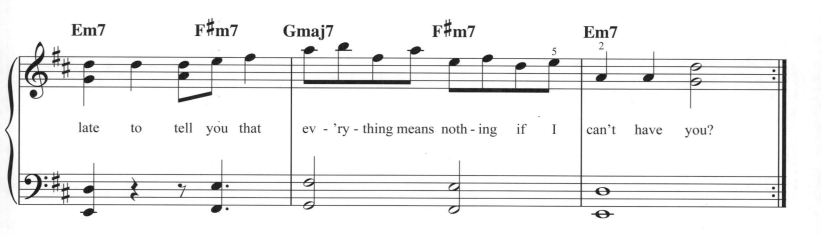

late to tell you that ev - 'ry - thing means noth - ing if I can't have you?

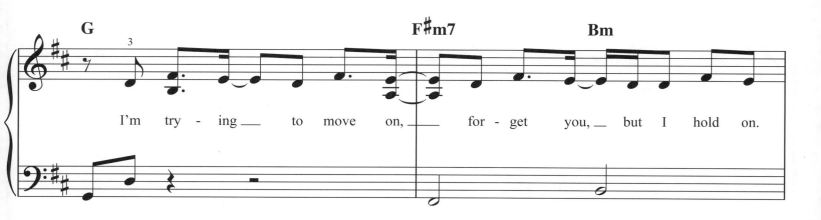

I'm try - ing __ to move on, __ for - get you, __ but I hold on.

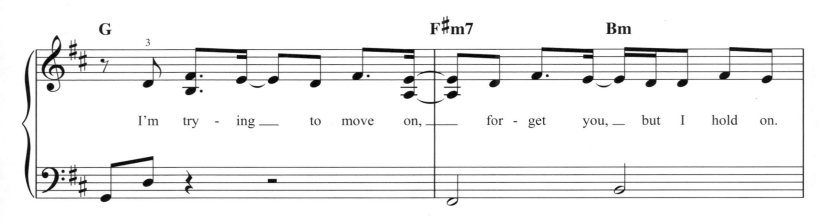

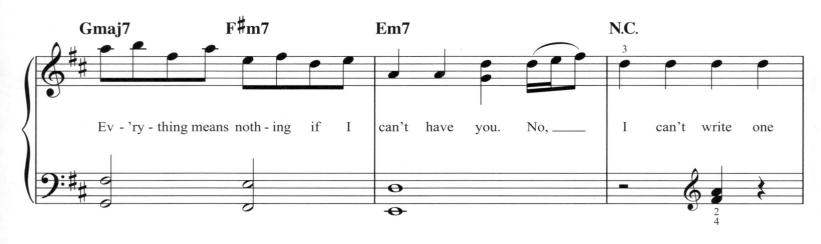

you.__ Is it too late to tell you that ev - 'ry - thing means noth - ing if I

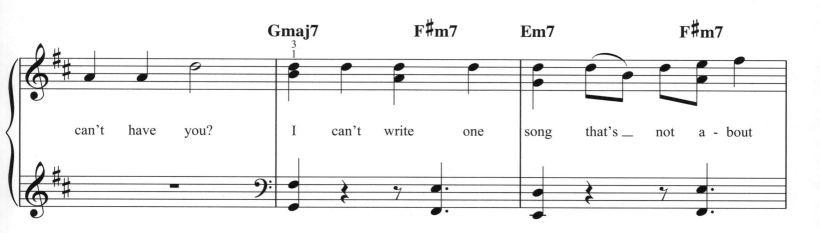

can't have you? I can't write one song that's __ not a - bout

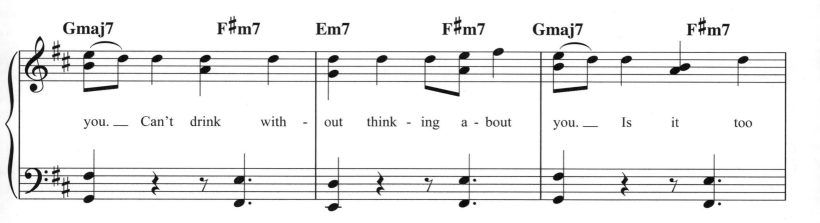

you.__ Can't drink with - out think - ing a - bout you.__ Is it too

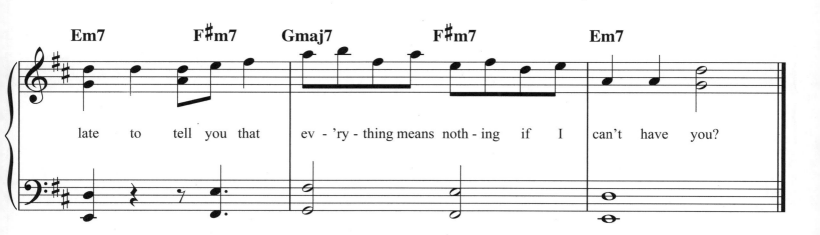

late to tell you that ev - 'ry - thing means noth - ing if I can't have you?

LO/HI

Words and Music by DAN AUERBACH
and PATRICK CARNEY

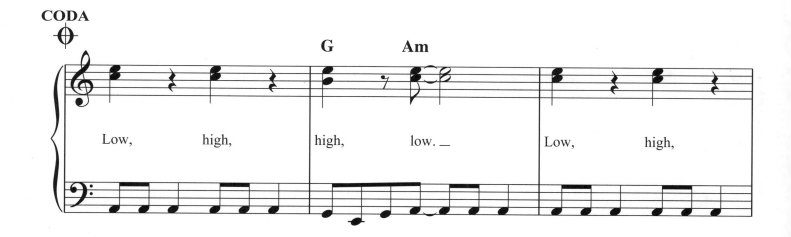

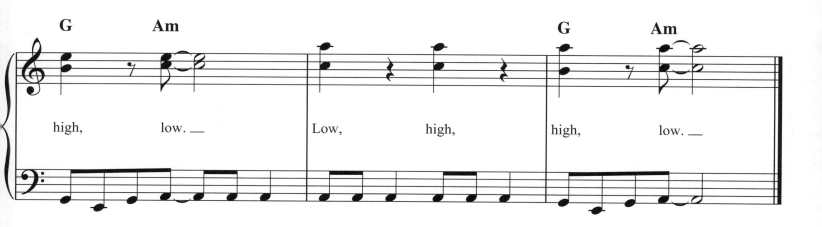

ME!

Words and Music by TAYLOR SWIFT,
JOEL LITTLE and BRENDON URIE

Moderately, in 2

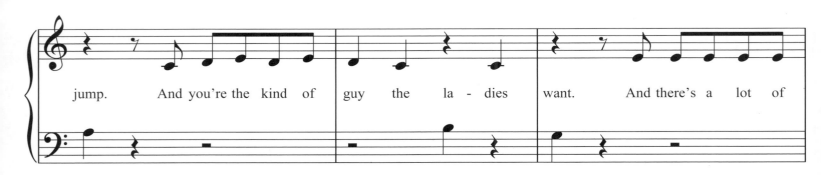

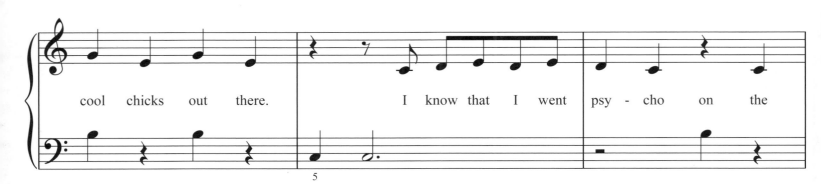

phone. I nev-er leave ___ well e-nough a - lone. And trou-ble's gon - na

fol - low where I go. And there's a lot of cool chicks out there. But

C

one of these things is not ___ like the oth - ers. Like a rain - bow with all ___

___ of the col - ors. Ba - by doll, when it comes ___ to a lov - er, I

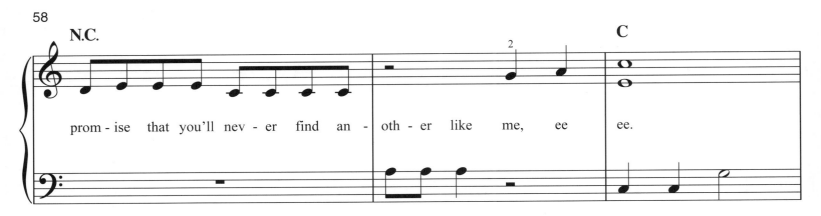

prom - ise   that   you'll   nev - er   find   an - oth - er   like   me,   ee   ee.

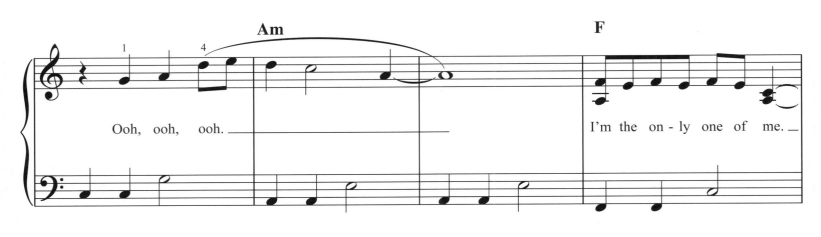

Ooh,   ooh,   ooh. _____   I'm the on - ly one of me. _____

Ba - by,   that's   the   fun   of   me,   ee   ee   ee. _____

Ooh,   ooh,   ooh. _____

You're the on - ly one of you.

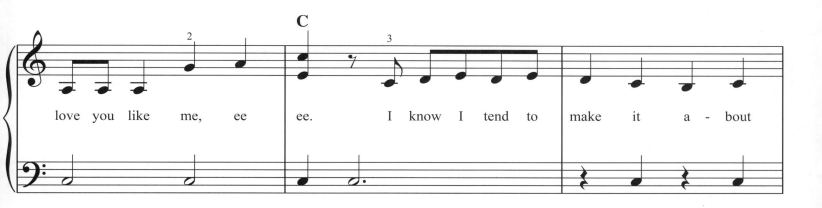

Ba - by, that's the fun of you. And I prom-ise that no-bod-y's gon - na

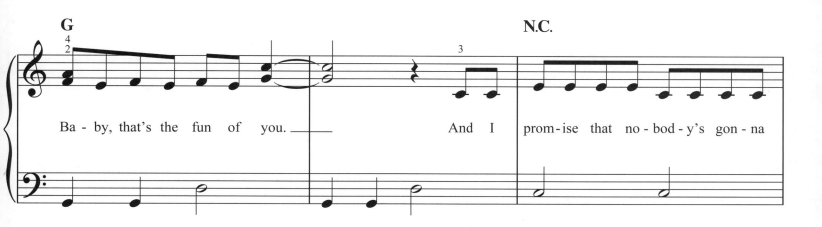

love you like me, ee ee. I know I tend to make it a - bout

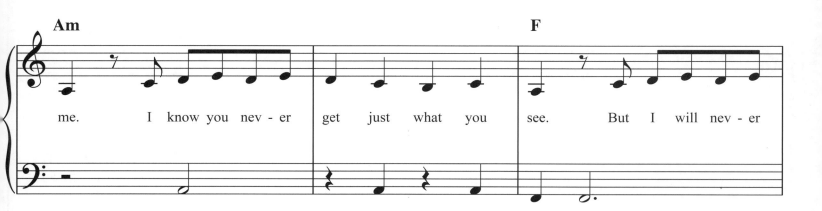

me. I know you nev - er get just what you see. But I will nev - er

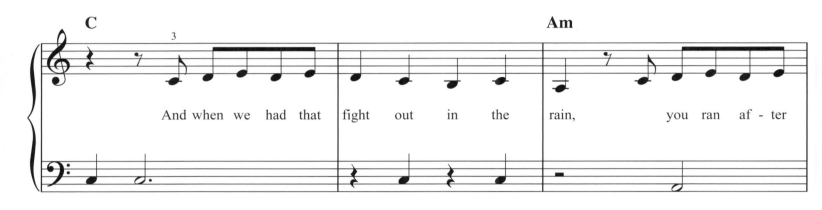

like the oth - ers. Liv - ing in win - ter, I ____ am your sum - mer.

Ba - by doll, when it comes ____ to a lov - er, I prom - ise that you'll nev - er find an -

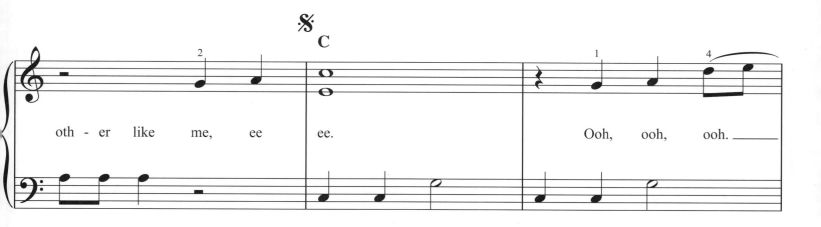

oth - er like me, ee ee. Ooh, ooh, ooh. ____

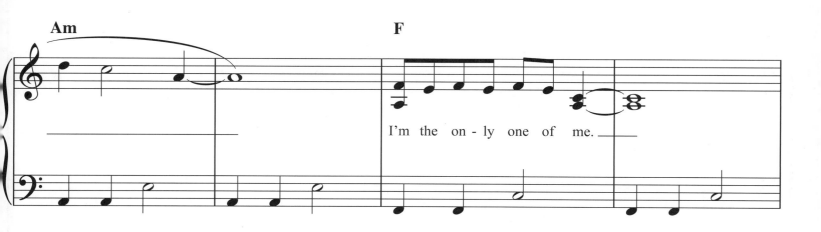

I'm the on - ly one of me. ____

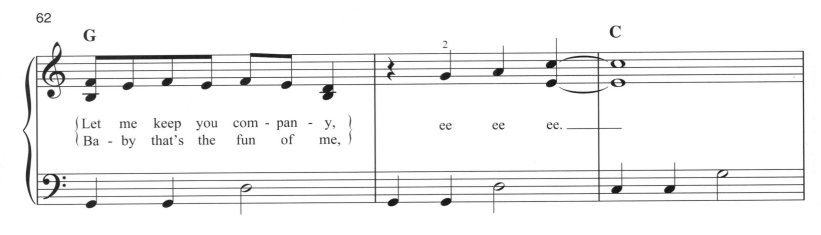

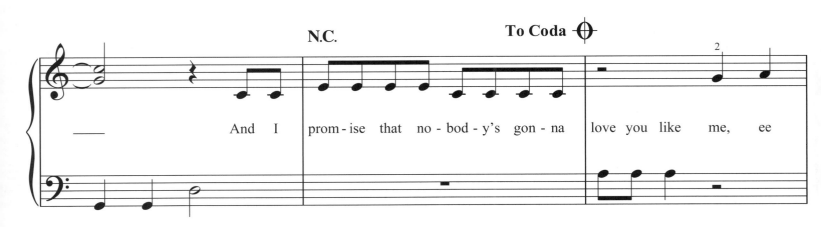

ee. Hey, kids, spell - ing is fun! Girl, there ain't no I____

____ in team. But you know there is____ a me. Strike the band up, one,____

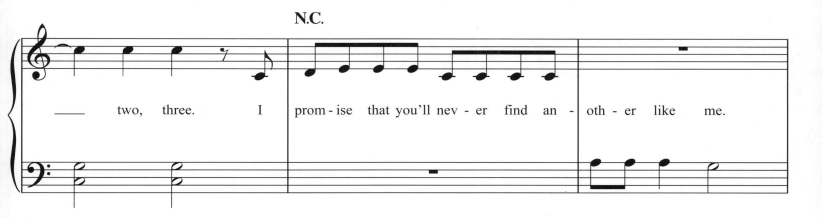

____ two, three. I prom - ise that you'll nev - er find an - oth - er like me.

Girl, there ain't no I____ in team. But you know there is____

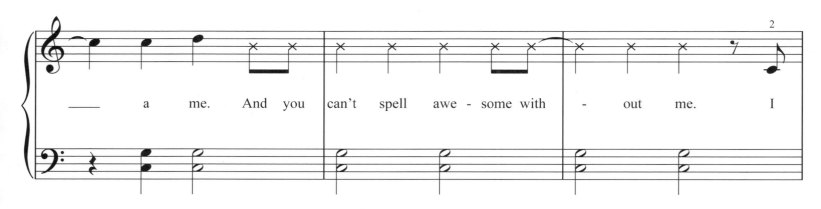

____ a me. And you can't spell awe - some with - out me. I

N.C.

prom-ise that you'll nev-er find an - oth-er like me, ee

D.S. al Coda

CODA

love you like me.

C

Girl, there ain't no I ____ in team.

Am

But you know there is ____

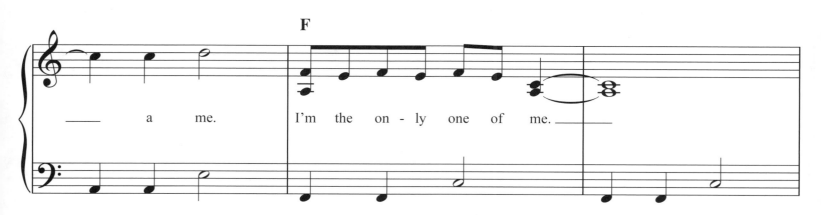

____ a me.

F

I'm the on - ly one of me. ____

Ba - by, that's the fun of me, ee ee ee. Strike the band up, one, __

__ two, three. You can't spell awe - some with - out me. __ You're the on - ly one of you. __

__ Ba - by, that's the fun of you. __ And I

prom - ise that no - bod - y's gon - na love you like me, ee ee.

NEVER REALLY OVER

Words and Music by KATY PERRY,
MICHELLE BUZZ, JASON GILL,
GINO BARLETTA, HAYLEY WARNER,
DAGNY SANDVIK, ANTON ZASLAVSKI,
LEAH HAYWOOD and DANIEL JAMES PRINGLE

Moderate Pop

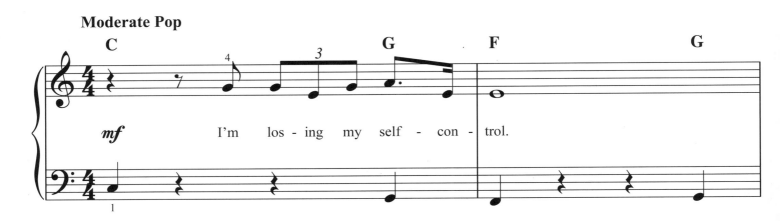

I'm los-ing my self-con-trol.

Yeah, you're start-ing to trick-le back in. ___

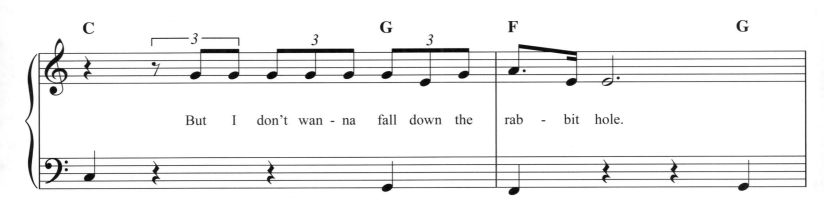

But I don't wan-na fall down the rab-bit hole.

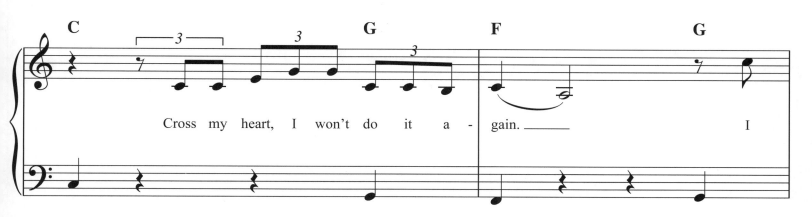

Cross my heart, I won't do it a - gain. _____ I

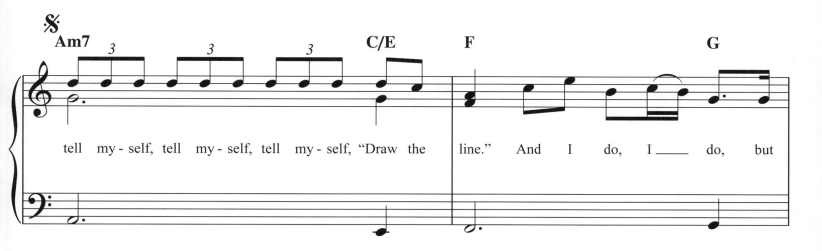

tell my - self, tell my - self, tell my - self, "Draw the line." And I do, I ___ do, but

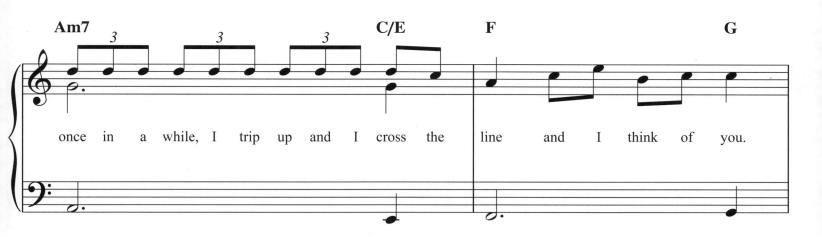

once in a while, I trip up and I cross the line and I think of you.

Two years and just like ___ that, my head still takes me ___ back.

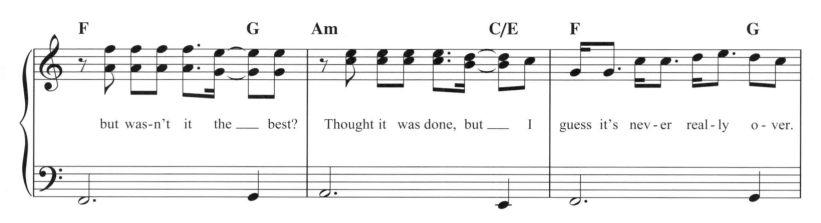

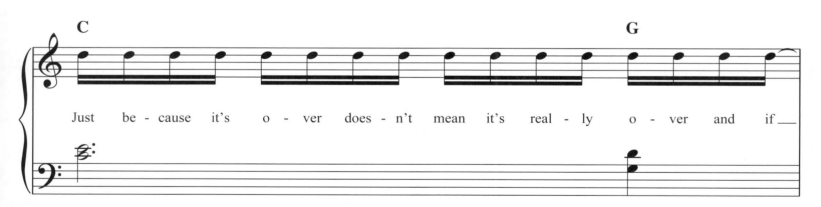

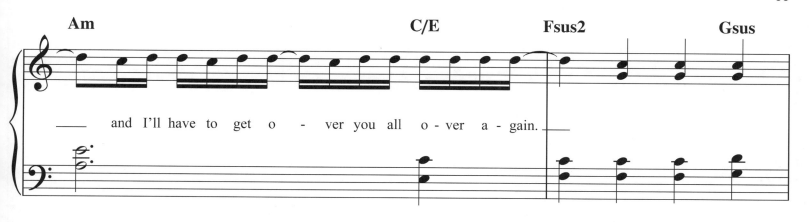

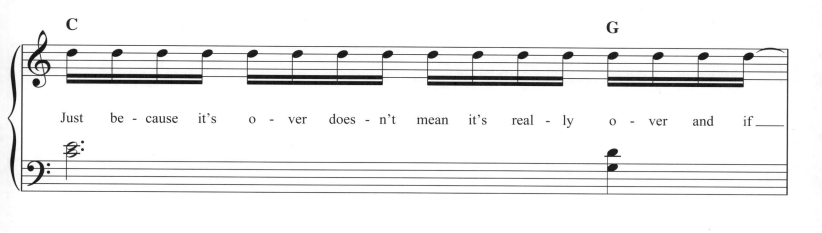

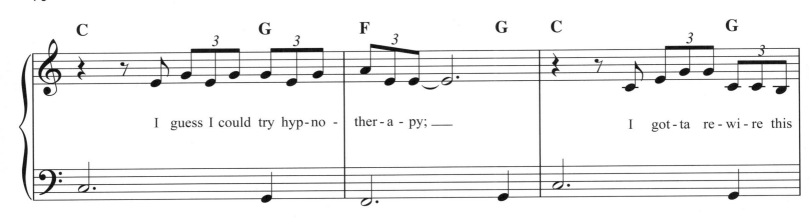

I guess I could try hyp-no - ther-a - py; — I got-ta re-wi-re this

brain. — 'Cause I can't e - ven go on the in - ter - net —

D.S. al Coda

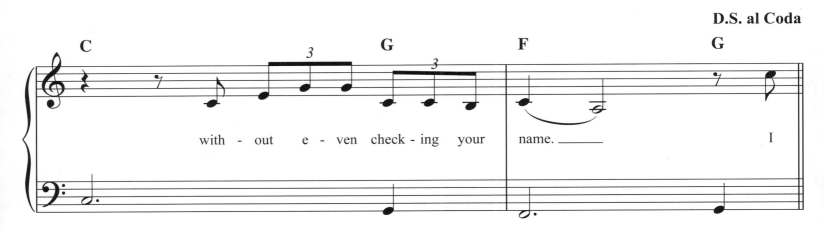

with - out e - ven check - ing your name. — I

CODA

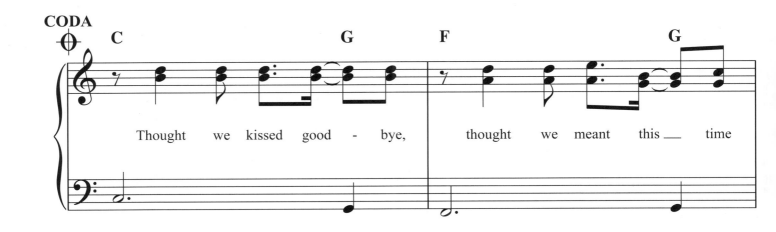

Thought we kissed good - bye, thought we meant this — time

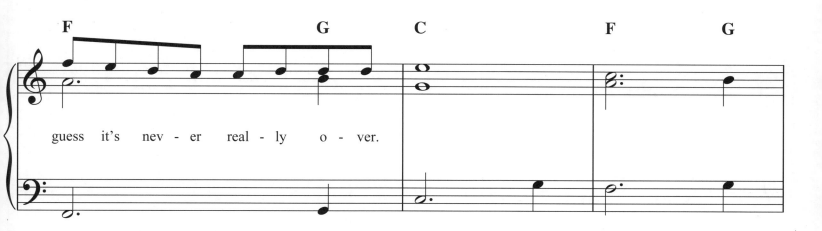

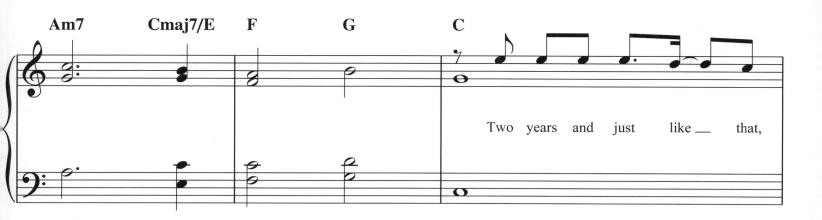

my head still takes me ___ back. Thought it was done, but ___ I guess it's nev-er real-ly o-ver.

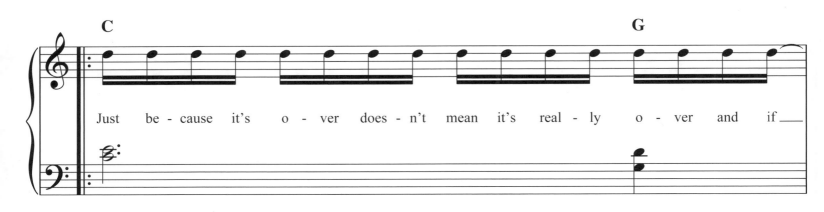

Just be-cause it's o-ver does-n't mean it's real-ly o-ver and if ___

___ I think it's o-ver, may-be you'll be com-ing o-ver a-gain, ___

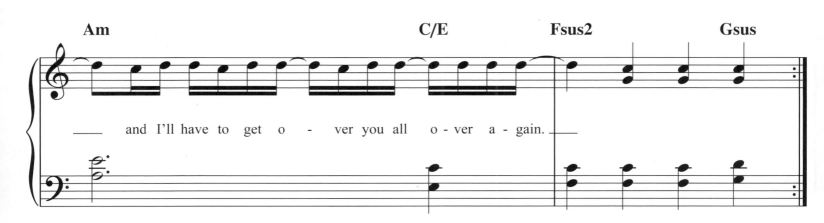

___ and I'll have to get o-ver you all o-ver a-gain.

Thought we kissed good - bye, thought we meant this ___ time was the last, but ___ I

guess it's nev - er real - ly o - ver. Thought we drew the ___ line right through you and ___ I.

Can't keep go - ing back I guess it's nev - er real - ly o - ver.

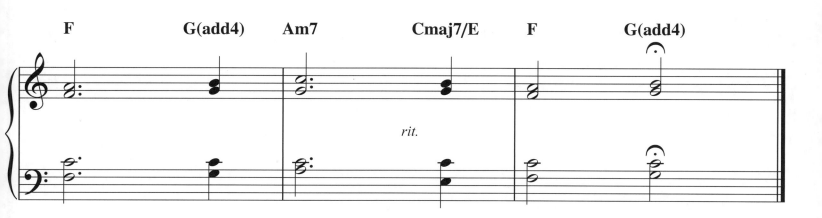

rit.

OLD TOWN ROAD
(Remix)

Words and Music by TRENT REZNOR,
BILLY RAY CYRUS, JOCELYN DONALD,
ATTICUS ROSS, KIOWA ROUKEMA
and MONTERO LAMAR HILL

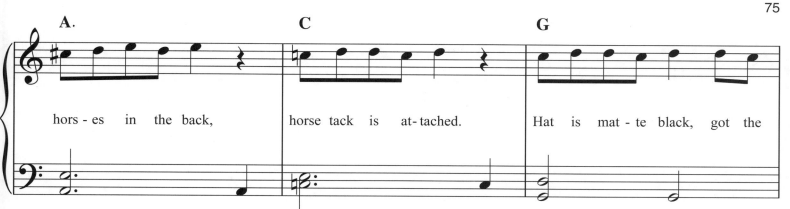

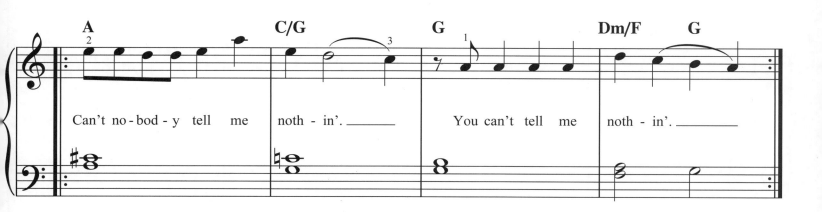

Rid-in' on a trac-tor, lean all in my blad-der. Cheat-ed on my ba-by,

you can go and ask — her. My life is a mov-ie, bull rid-in' and boob-ies.

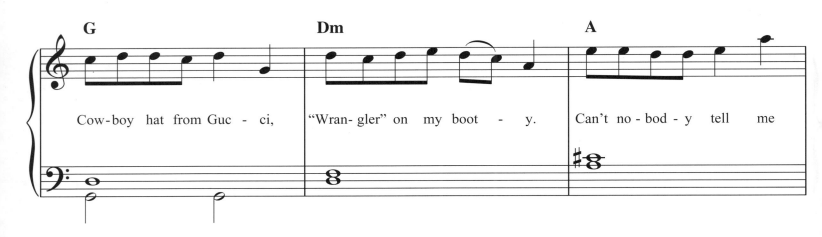

Cow-boy hat from Guc-ci, "Wran-gler" on my boot — y. Can't no-bod-y tell me

noth-in'. _____ You can't tell me noth-in'. _____ Can't no-bod-y tell me

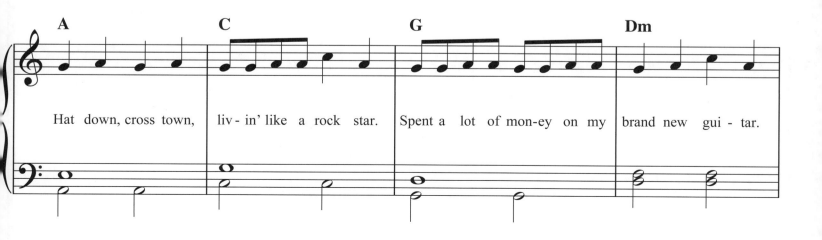

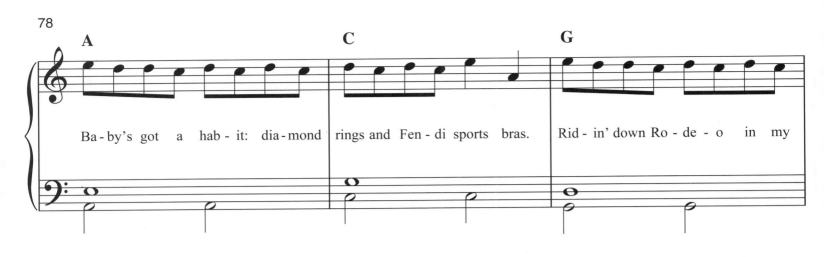

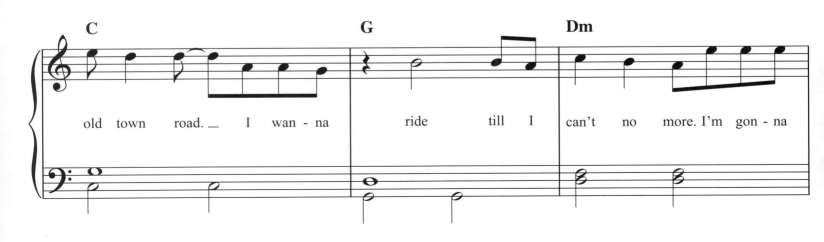

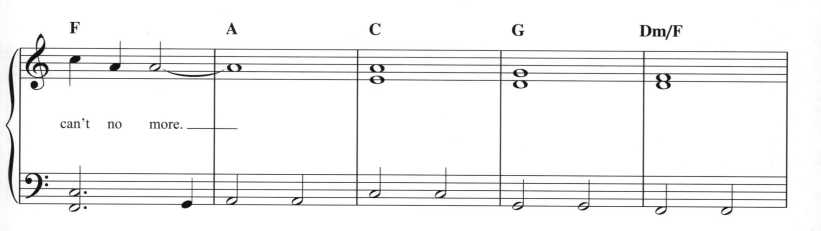

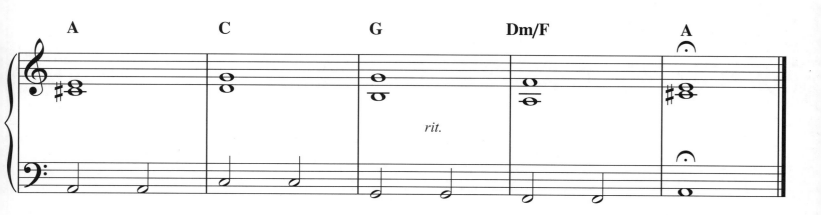

SEÑORITA

Words and Music by CAMILA CABELLO,
CHARLOTTE AITCHISON, JACK PATTERSON,
SHAWN MENDES, MAGNUS HOIBERG,
BENJAMIN LEVIN, ALI TAMPOSI
and ANDREW WOTMAN

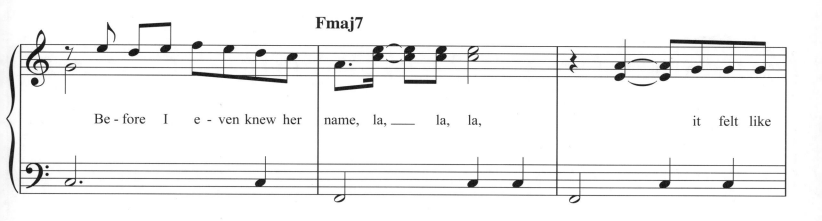

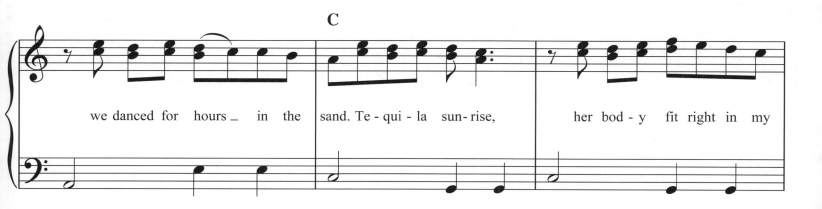

hands, la, ___ la, la. It felt like ooh, la, ___ la, la, yeah.

Both:
___ I love it when you call me "se-ño-ri - ta." I wish I could pre-

tend I did-n't need ___ ya, but ev-'ry touch is ooh, la, ___ la, la. It's

true, la, ___ la, la. Ooh, I should be run-nin'. Ooh, you know I love it when you

Am

call me "se - ño - ri - ta." I wish it was - n't

Cmaj7

so _____ hard to leave _____

_____ ya, but ev - 'ry touch is

F

ooh, la, _____ la, la. It's true, la, _____ la, la.

To Coda ⊕

Em

Ooh, I should be run - nin'.

Ooh, you keep me com - in' _____ for

Am

Female:
ya. Locked in the ho - tel,

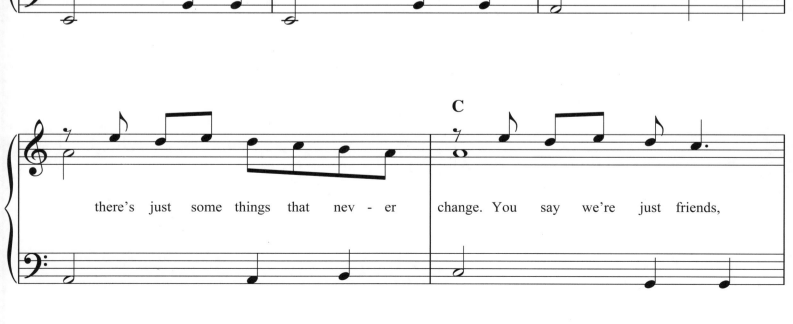

there's just some things that nev - er

C

change. You say we're just friends,

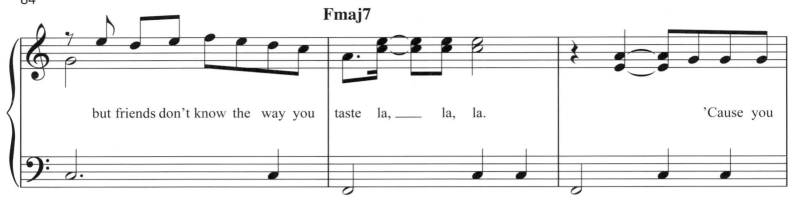

Fmaj7

but friends don't know the way you | taste la, ___ la, la. | 'Cause you

Em7   **G**

know it's been a long time com - in' don't you let me | fall, | oh. _____

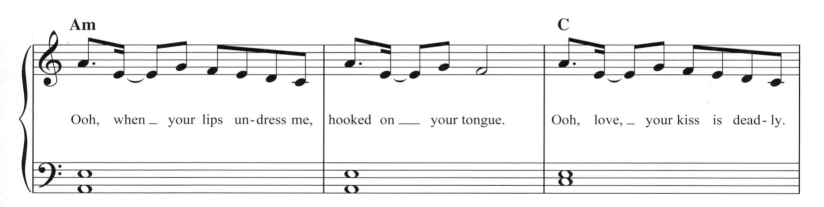

Am   **C**

Ooh, when ___ your lips un-dress me, | hooked on ___ your tongue. | Ooh, love, ___ your kiss is dead - ly.

G

D.S. al Coda

Both:
Don't stop. I love it when you

CODA

Am

ya. | All a - long I'll ___ be com - in' ___ for

ya.　　　　And I　hope　it ___ meant some - thin' ___ to　ya.　　　　Call my

name I'll ___ be com - in' ___ for │ ya.

Ooh,　I should be run- nin'. │ Ooh, you keep me com- in' ___ for │ ya.

SWEET BUT PSYCHO

Words and Music by AMANDA KOCI,
ANDREAS HAUKELAND, WILLIAM LOBBAN BEAN,
HENRY WALTER and MADISON LOVE

Moderately fast

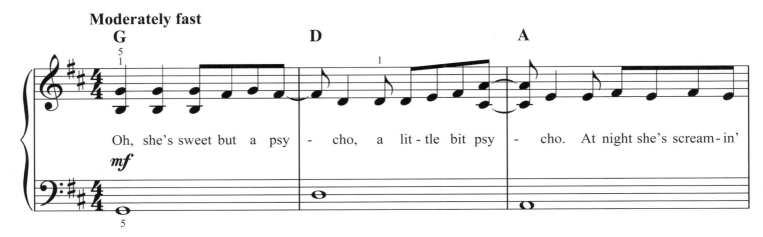

Oh, she's sweet but a psy - cho, a lit-tle bit psy - cho. At night she's scream-in'

"I'm-ma-ma out ___ my mind." ___ Oh, she's hot but a psy - cho. So left but she's right, ___

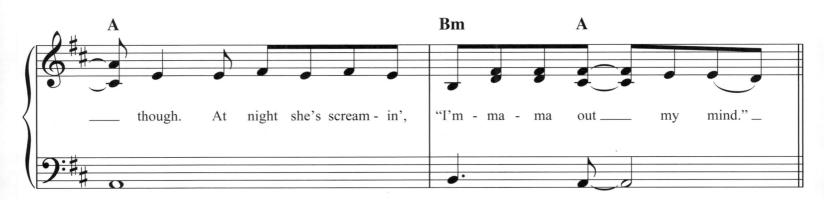

___ though. At night she's scream-in', "I'm-ma-ma out___ my mind." ___

"No, no," _____ then say - ing, "Yes, yes, _ yes" _ 'cause she mess - in'

with your _ head. _ Oh, she's sweet but a psy - cho, a lit - tle bit psy -

- cho. At night she's scream - in', "I'm - ma - ma out ____ my mind." _

Oh, she's hot but a psy - cho. So left but she's right, ____ though. At night she's scream - in',

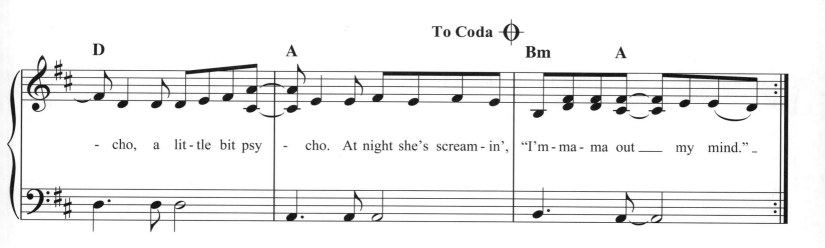

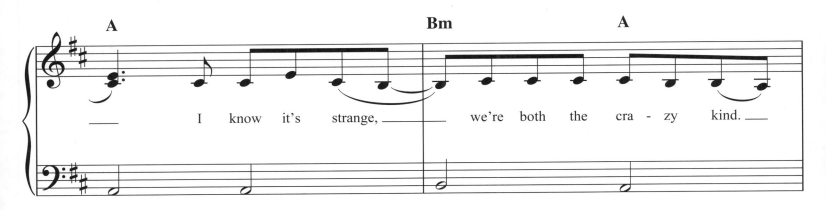

You're just like me, ____ you're out your mind. ____

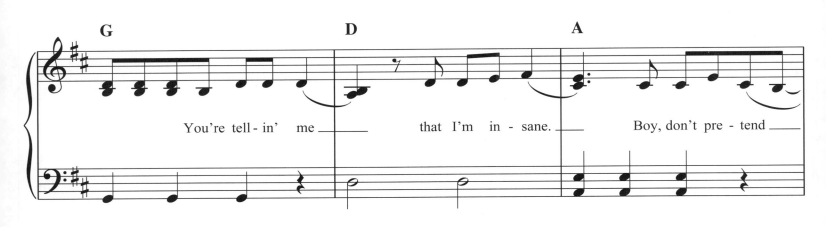

____ I know it's strange, ____ we're both the cra - zy kind. ____

Bm N.C. D.S. al Coda

____ that you don't love the pain. ____

CODA Bm N.C.

"I'm - ma - ma out ____ my mind." ____

SOMEONE YOU LOVED

Words and Music by LEWIS CAPALDI,
BENJAMIN KOHN, PETER KELLEHER
THOMAS BARNES and SAMUEL ROMAN

Moderate Ballad

I'm go-ing un-der, and this time I fear there's no one to save ___
I'm go-ing un-der, and this time I fear there's no one to turn ___

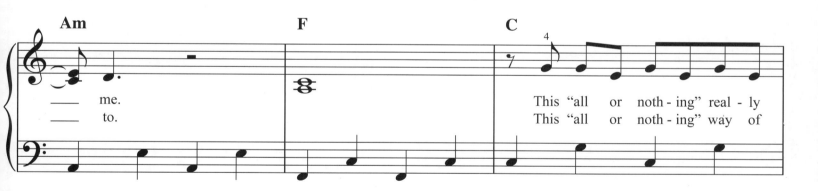

__ me.   This "all or noth-ing" real-ly
__ to.   This "all or noth-ing" way of

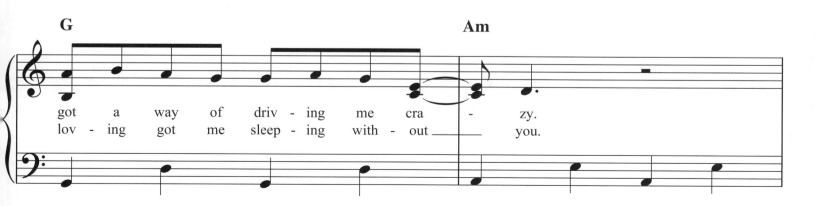

got a way of driv-ing me cra - zy.
lov-ing got me sleep-ing with-out ___ you.

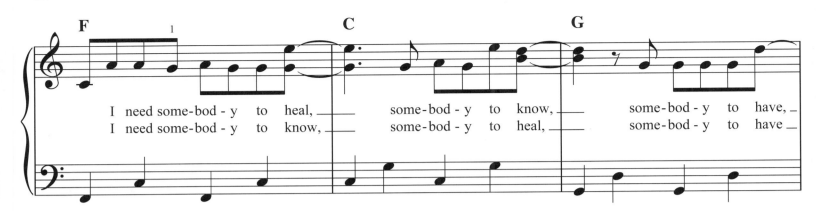

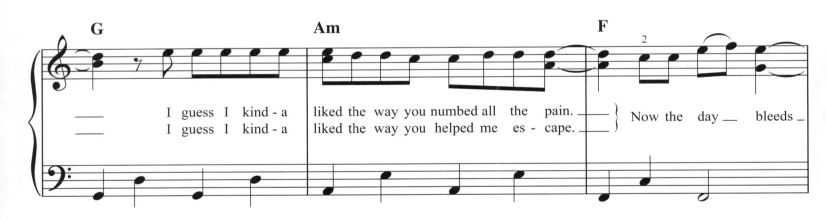

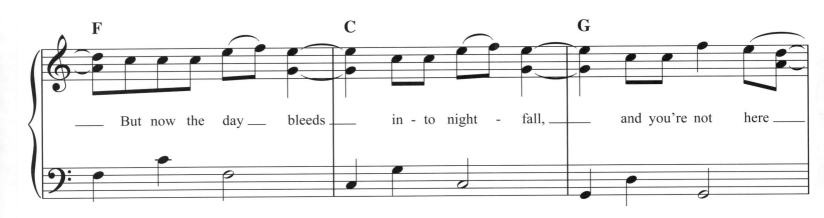

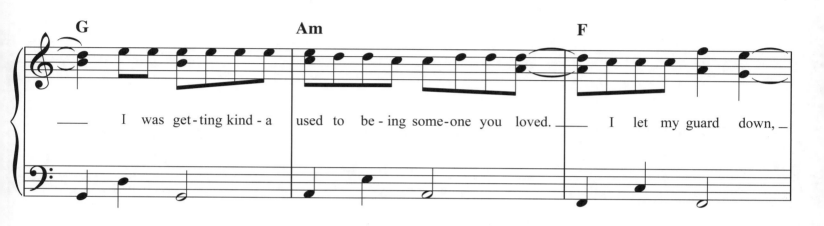

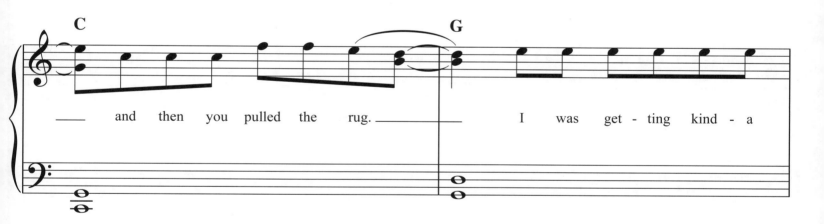

SPEECHLESS

from ALADDIN

Music by ALAN MENKEN
Lyrics by BENJ PASEK
and JUSTIN PAUL

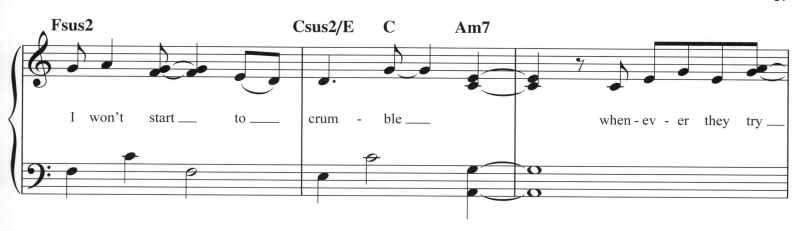

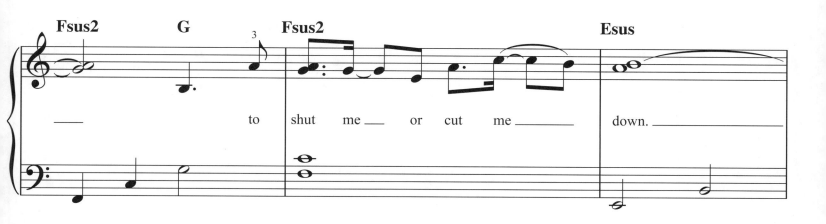

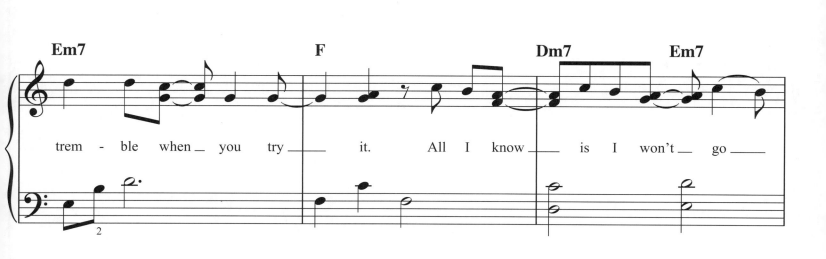

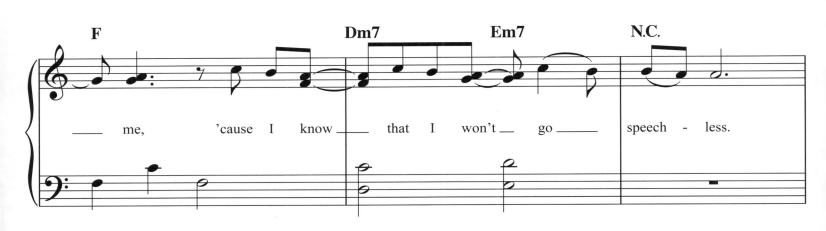

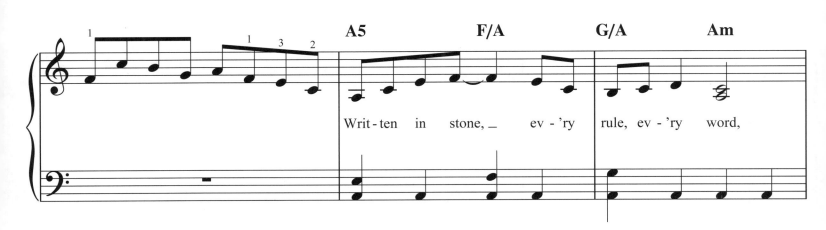

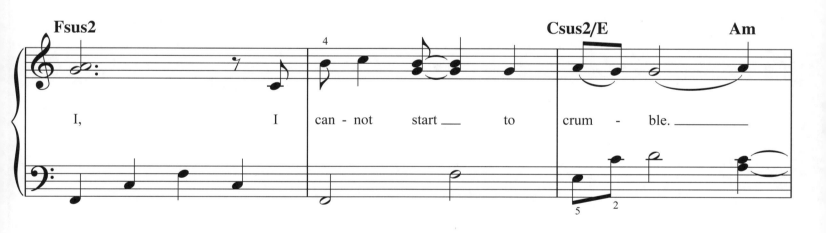

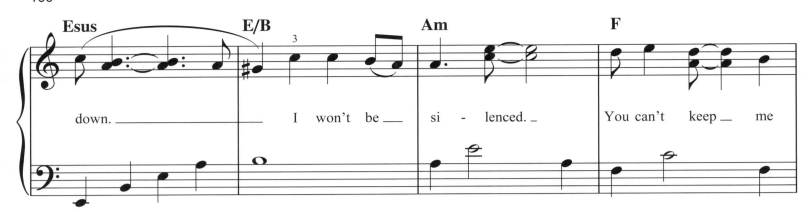

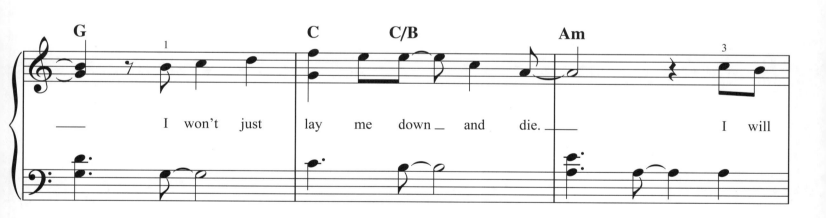

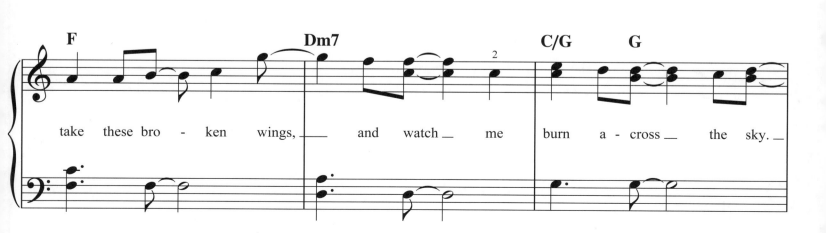

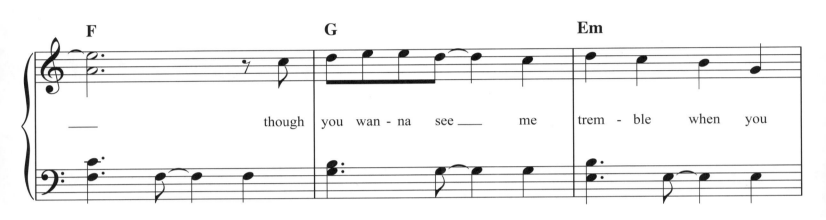

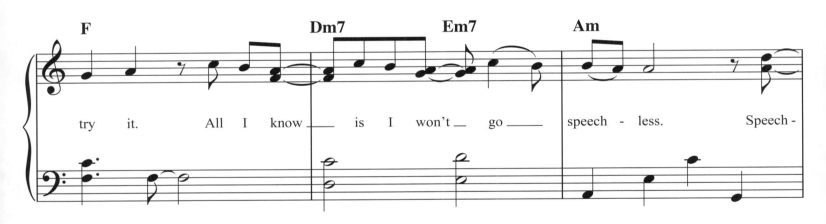

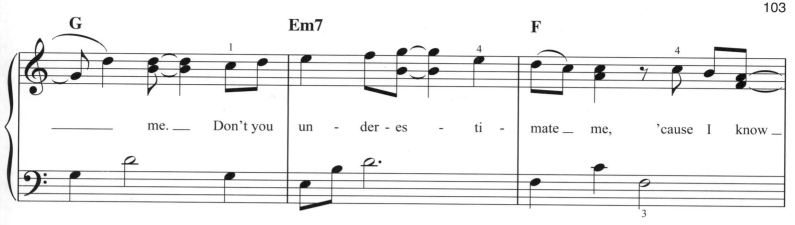

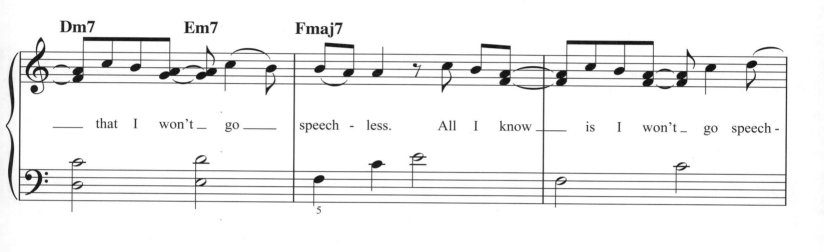

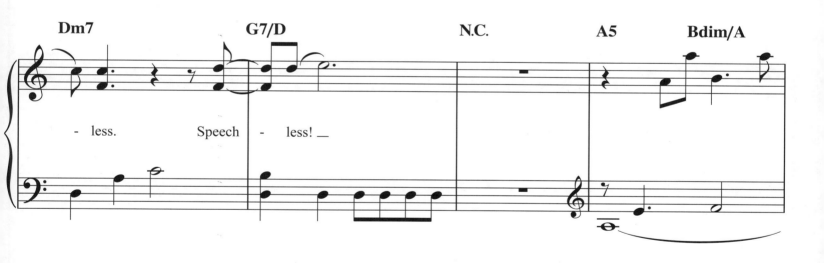

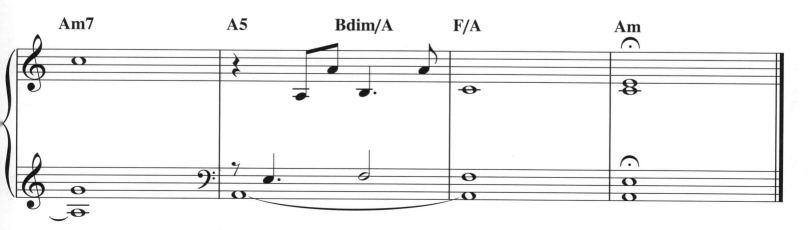

SUCKER

Words and Music by NICK JONAS,
JOSEPH JONAS, MILES ALE,
RYAN TEDDER, LOUIS BELL,
ADAM FEENEY and KEVIN JONAS

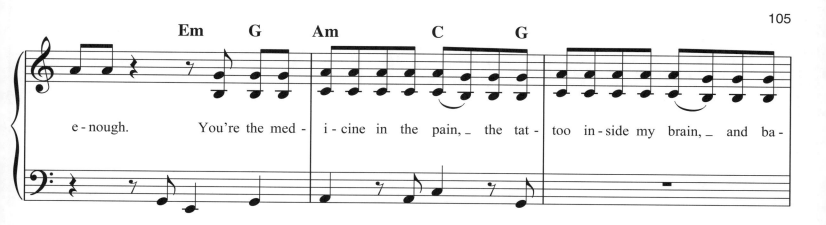

e - nough. You're the med - i - cine in the pain, _ the tat - too in - side my brain, _ and ba-

by, you know it's ob - vi - ous: I'm a suck - er for you. _

Say the word and I'll go an - y-where blind - ly. _____ I'm a suck - er for you, _

_____ yeah. _____ An - y road you take, you know that you'll find me. _____

I'm a suck-er for all the sub-lim-i-nal things ___ no one knows a-bout

you, (a-bout you) a-bout you (a-bout you). And you're mak-ing the typ-i-cal me ___

To Coda ⊕

___ break my typ-i-cal rules. ___ It's true, I'm a suck-er for

1.

you.   Don't com-pli-

2.

you.

I've been danc -

you.

I'm a suck - er for you.

TALK

Words and Music by KHALID ROBINSON, GUY LAWRENCE and HOWARD LAWRENCE

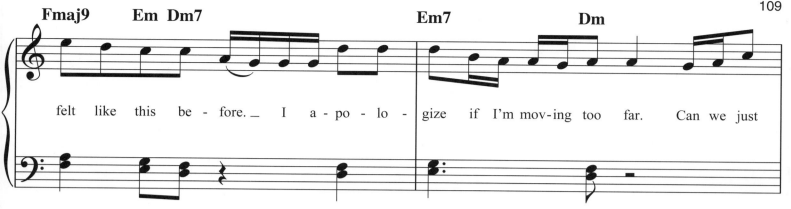

felt like this be - fore. _ I a - po - lo - gize if I'm mov-ing too far. Can we just

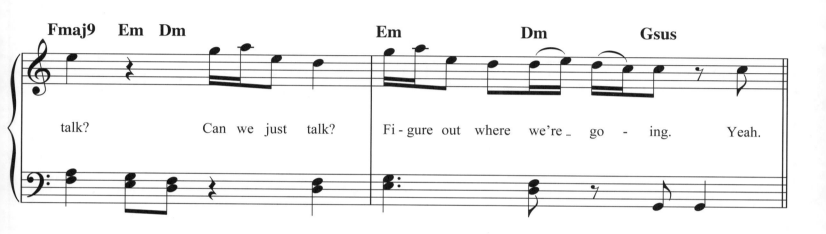

talk?   Can we just talk?   Fi - gure out where we're _ go - ing.   Yeah.

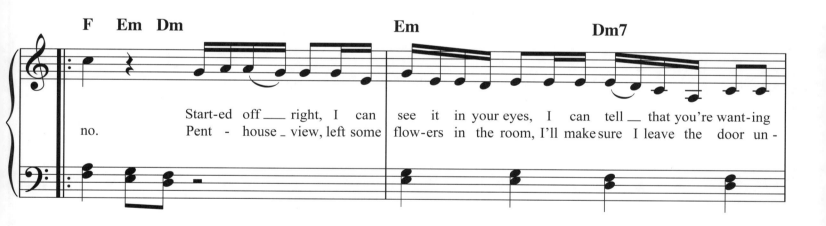

Start-ed off __ right, I can   see it in your eyes, I can tell _ that you're want-ing

no.   Pent - house _ view, left some   flow-ers in the room, I'll make sure I leave the door un -

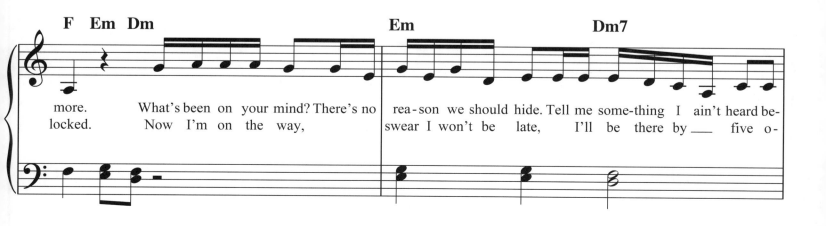

more.   What's been on your mind? There's no   rea-son we should hide. Tell me some-thing I ain't heard be-

locked.   Now I'm on the way,   swear I won't be late, I'll be there by __ five o-

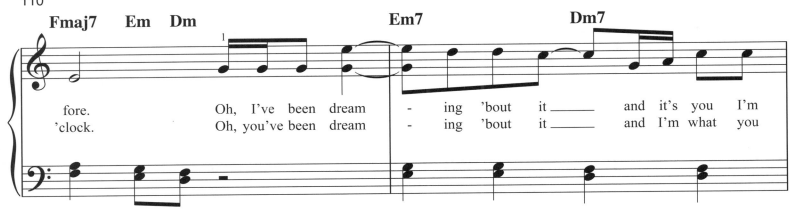

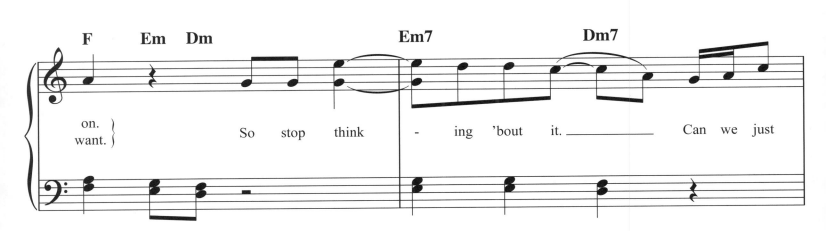

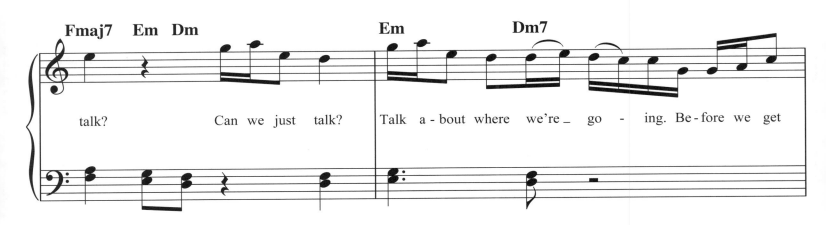

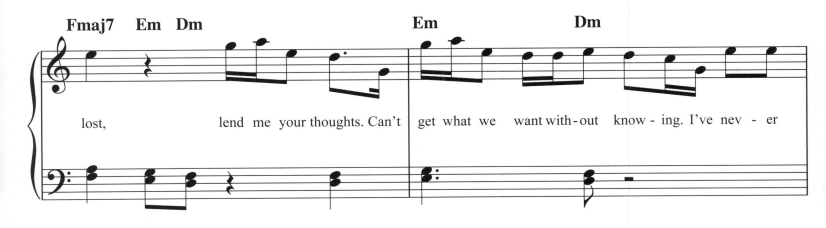

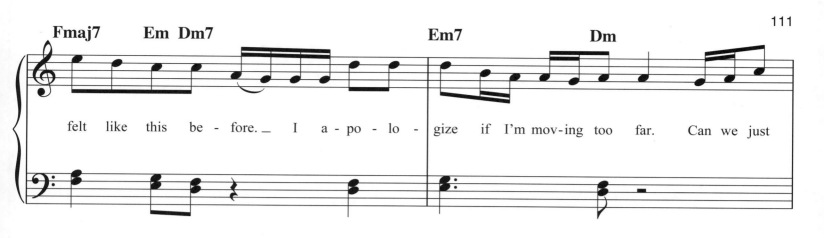

felt like this be - fore.__ I a - po - lo - gize if I'm mov-ing too far. Can we just

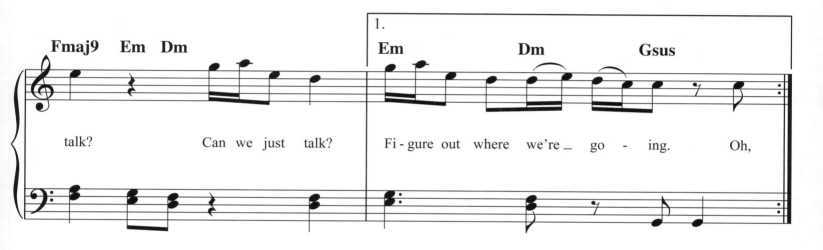

talk? Can we just talk? Fi - gure out where we're__ go - ing. Oh,

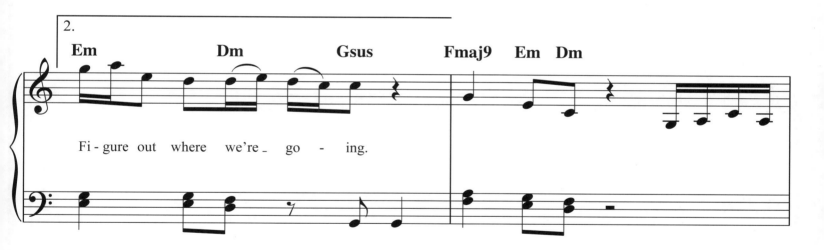

Fi - gure out where we're__ go - ing.

WALK ME HOME

Words and Music by ALECIA MOORE,
SCOTT HARRIS and NATE RUESS

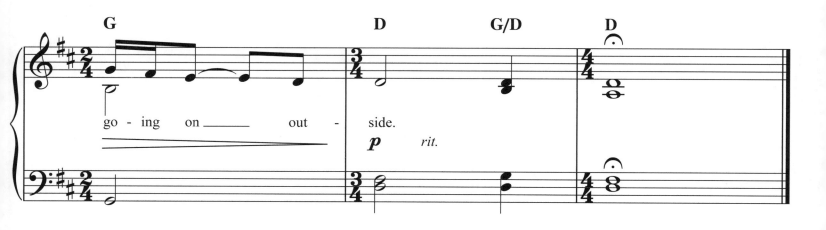

YOU NEED TO CALM DOWN

Words and Music by TAYLOR SWIFT
and JOEL LITTLE

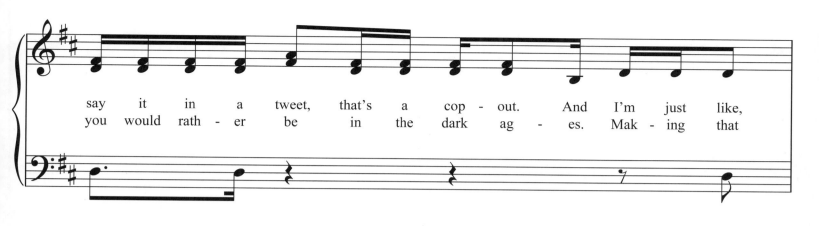

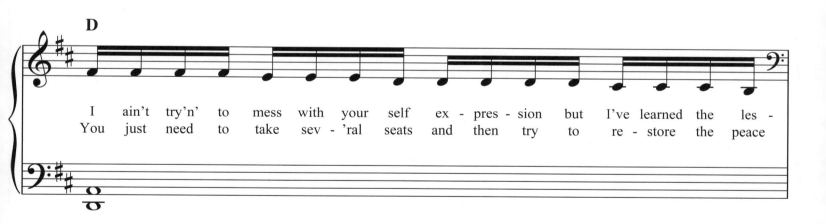

D

down. (Oh, oh, oh, oh, oh, oh, oh, oh.) ___ You need to calm

G

down. ___ You're be-ing too loud. ___ And I'm just like,

D

oh, oh, (Oh, oh, oh, oh, oh, oh, oh, oh.) ___ you need to just

G   **D**

stop. ___ Like, can you just not ___ step on our gowns? You need to calm down.